SOCIAL WORK AND LAW

HOUSING: REPAIRS
AND
IMPROVEMENTS

AUSTRALIA

The Law Book Company Ltd.
Sydney : Melbourne : Brisbane

CANADA AND U.S.A.

The Carswell Company Ltd.
Agincourt, Ontario

INDIA

N.M. Tripathi Private Ltd.
Bombay
and
Eastern Law House Private Ltd.
Calcutta
M.P.P. House
Bangalore

ISRAEL

Steimatzky's Agency Ltd.
Jerusalem : Tel Aviv : Haifa

MALAYSIA : SINGAPORE : BRUNEI

Malayan Law Journal (Pte.) Ltd.
Singapore

NEW ZEALAND

Sweet and Maxwell (N.Z.) Ltd.
Wellington

PAKISTAN

Pakistan Law House
Karachi

SOCIAL WORK AND LAW

HOUSING: REPAIRS AND IMPROVEMENTS

by

TOM HADDEN

LONDON
SWEET & MAXWELL
1979

Published in 1979 by
Sweet & Maxwell Ltd. of
11 New Fetter Lane, London
Photoset by Red Lion Setters, London
Printed in Great Britain by
Richard Clay (The Chaucer Press), Ltd.,
Bungay, Suffolk

ISBN 0 421 23810 0

Preface

Bad housing may be portrayed as a legal problem — the result of failure by a landlord or a local authority to perform a legal duty. The purpose of a book on housing repairs and improvements on that view would be to explain what those legal duties are and how they may be enforced. There are obvious attractions in such an approach from the point of view of those working in legal advice centres, in social work departments and even in local authorities.

In practice it is not as simple as that. A good deal may be achieved by a tough legal rights approach to house repair and improvement. But, as will be seen, the law in this sphere is rarely expressed in absolute terms. There is no right to a reasonable standard of housing in any strict legal sense. Housing legislation is a mixture of qualified individual rights and complex administrative provisions through which it is intended that local authorities and central government should act to improve housing conditions generally within the limits of the financial resources available. Much of the law gives *discretionary powers* to local authorities to secure repairs and improvements in appropriate cases rather than *absolute rights* to individuals.

This book is designed to reflect that basic fact. The rights and duties of individual tenants and owners are outlined and the methods of enforcement explained. But equal attention is paid to the more general issues of housing policy and administration, and the assistance which individuals may in practice expect to receive from their local authorities.

The first two chapters are accordingly devoted to an explanation of the problem of bad housing, its underlying causes, and the development of housing legislation over the past hundred years or so. Since action to improve housing conditions is so often dependent on discretionary decisions by local government officials and councillors it is important to understand the framework within which the various legal procedures must be approached, and in particular the allocation of functions between Environmental Health (Public Health) Departments and Housing Departments. Though many of the powers and duties of those two departments, derived primarily from the Public Health Acts and the Housing Acts respectively, are now increasingly co-ordinated, the traditions and underlying assumptions of each remain sufficiently different to make it important for individual tenants and owners and their advisers to distinguish between them.

The remaining chapters are devoted to a more detailed analysis and explanation of the law and its practical administration on specific topics. Chapter 3 deals with the allocation of duties of repair and maintenance between landlords and tenants both under the common law and under the Housing Acts, and with the enforcement of those duties in the county courts or by self-help. Chapter 4 deals with the enforcement of repair and improvement through the statutory procedures provided in the Public Health and Housing Acts. Chapter 5 deals with the various forms of repair and improvement grants currently available to owners and the conditions which local authorities may impose before approving them. Chapter 6 deals with the additional powers and procedures governing the provision of facilities and the prevention of overcrowding in houses in multiple occupation. Chapter 7 contains a more general account of the use of all the various powers in areas specifically designated for improvement or rehabilitation, notably in Housing Action Areas (HAAs) declared under the Housing Act 1974. Finally in Chapter 8 a brief account is given of the relevant aspects of the law on compulsory purchase, rehousing and compensation for those displaced by redevelopment or rehabilitation.

In all these chapters the main emphasis is on the practical application of the various interlocking rights, duties and procedures and on the different standpoints of individual tenants, owners and local authority officials. The objective throughout is to give a realistic and down to earth account of what can be achieved and what is unlikely to be achieved for all those who are concerned with the repair and improvement of poor quality housing, from individual tenants, landlords and owner-occupiers to officials in local authority departments and in central government. To assist in this a series of standard form documents has been provided in the appendices, and in addition a more precise discussion of some of the more complex legal and practical issues involved, notably the items which local authorities may be prepared to treat as improvements, and the operation of the reasonable expense criterion which governs a number of compulsory repair and improvement procedures.

It will be clear to anyone who attempts to master all these separate but often interlocking powers and procedures that housing law in this sphere is confused and sometimes inconsistent. In the concluding chapter a brief account is given of the way in which the existing law might be reformed and codified to provide a more straightforward and effective legal framework for the maintenance, repair and improvement of older houses. This chapter is directed primarily at those concerned with the development of housing policy and the preparation of new legislation. It is based largely on my research report on the operation of compulsory repair and improvement procedures under the Housing Acts 1957 and 1974, carried out in the latter part of 1977 at the SSRC Centre for Socio-Legal Studies, Wolfson College, Oxford. The report was published in 1978 under the title *Compulsory Repair and Improvement: a study of the operation of the Housing Acts 1957 and 1974.*

While this book was being written there was continuing uncertainty over the prospects for a new Housing Bill. The outgoing Labour government eventually published its Bill in March 1979, but further progress was thwarted by the dissolution of Parliament. Some at least of the contents of that Bill, however, are non-contentious and seem likely to be adopted by any future government. Brief reference has therefore been made to relevant provisions on tenancy agreements and on grants in Chapters 3 and 5. Despite concerted pressure from a number of interested bodies no provisions were included for the simplification of compulsory improvement procedures.

I am grateful for assistance and useful comments from the

following: George Allan, Andrew Arden, N. Boga (London Borough of Islington), Alan Chapman (London Borough of Brent), Alison Curtis (Queen's University), Frank Bird (Leicester City Council), Keith Davies (University of Reading), Paddy Hillyard (University of Bristol), Judy Kelly (University of British Columbia), Gillian Lomas (Centre for Environmental Studies), John McCarthy (Department of the Environment), Robert McKay (Sweet and Maxwell), Chris Moffat (Lloyd-Baker Institute), Elizabeth Monck (Centre for Environmental Studies), David Ormandy (Public Health Advisory Service), Harry Page (Bristol City Council), Chris Paris (Centre for Environmental Studies), Martin Partington (London School of Economics), John Perry (Leicester City Council), Len Quartly (Birmingham City Council), Hilary Robinson (National Consumer Council) and Adrian Taylor (University of Kent at Canterbury). Rosemary Jack deserves particular thanks for her imaginative drawings. I am also grateful for permission from the Consumers Association to reproduce extracts from their report on grants, from the National Consumer Council to reproduce extracts from their model tenancy agreement, and from the Public Health Advisory Service to draw on and develop their set of draft letters for various types of enforcement.

Derrybroughas,   Tom Hadden
Portadown
Easter Day 1979

TABLE OF CONTENTS

TABLE OF CASES

References are given to the most accessible reports of cases referred to in the text; the abbreviations used are as follows

TABLE OF STATUTES

1 The Problem of Bad Housing

The housing problem is usually portrayed as one of shortage: too many people chasing too few houses. In reality there have usually been almost enough houses to go round. In the past few years the number of houses in Britain has actually exceeded the number of households. The really serious problem, except in the aftermath of the wars of 1914-18 and 1939-45, has been bad housing rather than lack of housing. At any one time the number of homeless people has been only a tiny proportion of the number of people living in poor quality accommodation.

A few simple figures taken from the Housing Policy Review of 1977 (Cmnd. 6851) will bear out these claims. It was reckoned that in 1976 there were more than 18 million houses in England and Wales and only 17½ million households, making a crude surplus of about half a million houses. The number of families officially regarded as homeless in 1975 was only about 50,000. But the number of houses officially classified as unfit for human habitation in England and Wales in 1976 was some 900,000, and a further 800,000 were recorded as lacking one of the basic amenities. More than three million houses were reckoned to require repairs costing more than £500.

The implication of figures like these is not that more new houses are not required. Bad housing and housing shortage are two sides of the same coin. People in bad houses are often on the look out for somewhere better. Too many people crammed into a perfectly good house can soon turn it into a slum. It was reckoned that in 1976 some 150,000 households were living in overcrowded accommodation and that another million were sharing accommodation. If only a small proportion of the people who are currently in poor quality or overcrowded houses wanted to be rehoused, the apparent surplus of half a million houses would be turned into a huge deficit. Many of the surplus houses are in any event situated in parts of the country where people do not want to live or cannot find jobs. Quite apart from this, an increasing number of newly formed families want a home of their own immediately, and many elderly people now prefer to live on their own rather than share with relatives. Then there are those who want second homes or already have them. As standards and expectations rise there will always be a shortage of good quality housing.

1. *Who is Badly Housed?*

Crude figures always conceal as much as they clarify. Bad housing is unevenly distributed among the three main sectors: owner occupation, council housing and privately rented housing. More than half the houses in England today are owner-occupied, compared with about one third council houses and one sixth privately rented. But as the table shows, more than half the unfit houses in 1976 were in the private rented sector, in which roughly one in six of the houses were unfit; this compared with figures of one in 30 for owner-occupied houses and one in a hundred for council houses.

Table 1.1
The Distribution of Houses and Unfit Houses between
the Three Main Sectors, England 1976

	No. of houses	% of total stock	No. unfit	% of sector unfit
Owner-occupied	9.5m	56%	263,000	3%
Council houses	4.8m	28%	46,000	1%
Privately rented	2.3m	13%	334,000	15%
Vacant	0.5m	3%	151,000	30%
Total stock	17.1m	100%	794,000	5%

Source: English House Condition 1976.

It is easy to deduce from figures like these that the main problem is bad landlords. Even that is too simple a conclusion. There is a direct and obvious relationship between the age of a house and the likelihood of its being unfit or in bad repair.

But the older houses are not evenly distributed between the three sectors, not least because almost all the new houses built since the 1930s have been either for owner-occupiers or else council houses. The result is that the proportion of pre-1919 houses in the private rented sector is very much higher (70 per cent) than in the owner-occupied sector (31 per cent) or the public sector (4 per cent) (1976 figures). If this is taken into account, a very different picture of the underlying causes of unfitness emerges. As shown in Table 1.2, virtually all the unfit houses were built before 1919, and the differences in the proportion of those in the owner-occupied, public and private rented sectors which are unfit is much less striking. Only about one in 10 of the owner-occupied houses were unfit; but three in 10 of both public and private rented houses were unfit (1976 figures).

Table 1.2
The Distribution of Unfit Houses Built Before and After 1919
between the Three Main Sectors, England 1976

	Pre-1919			1919-1976		
	Total houses	*No. unfit*	*% unfit*	*Total houses*	*No. unfit*	*% unfit*
Owner-occupied	2.9m	256,000	9%	6.7m	7,000	0.1%
Council houses	0.2m	38,000	21%	4.6m	8,000	0.2%
Private rented	1.6m	324,000	21%	0.7m	10,000	1.4%
Vacant	0.3m	143,000	41%	0.2m	8,000	5.3%
Total stock	5.0m	761,000	15%	12.2m	33,000	0.3%

Source: English House Condition Survey 1976.

There are a number of other factors which must also be taken into account. In the first place there is a substantial difference in urban and rural conditions. Many older rural houses are technically unfit, but would not be considered at all unsatisfactory by the families that live in them. One man's idyllic cottage is a public health inspector's slum. Many fewer of these houses are in potential clearance or rehabilitation areas than in the towns and cities, and are likely to remain a statistical if not a practical problem. In the second place the designation of houses as fit and unfit is a variable and some-times highly arbitrary matter. The statutory definition of unfitness in terms of suitability for occupation, as will be seen, leaves a great deal to the discretion of the inspecting officer. Different standards are applied in different areas, and for different purposes. If a local authority is embarking on a slum clearance programme, it is likely to set a high standard for fitness, if only to reduce the level of compensation it must pay to owners and landlords. If it is inspecting its own properties, on the other hand, it may set a much lower standard for fitness, to avoid the opprobrium of reporting high levels of unfitness and the consequent duty to rehouse occupants. Many people think that the condition of some older council houses and high rise blocks makes them just as unsuitable for occupation as houses which are designated as unfit in the private sector. It is always dangerous to take officially compiled statistics at their face value, without inquiring in more detail into the way in which they have been compiled.

Even when all these factors — the distribution of older houses, the urban/rural problem and the inherent uncertainty and variability of classifications — it remains a fact that the worst housing conditions are often concentrated in privately rented houses and flats in inner city areas. Before considering the nature and merits of current housing law and policy it is important to look briefly at some of the underlying causes for this pattern.

2.   *The Economics of Bad Housing*

The principal explanation for the concentration of bad housing in the private rented sector is the pattern of investment in housing. During the nineteenth century most housebuilding was undertaken by mill and factory owners, or by property owners on their behalf, to provide cheap accommodation for their workers. Though some of these terraces were of good quality, many were built to very low standards. Most of the terraced housing in our cities and towns was provided in this way. In 1919 nine in every 10 households rented their houses from private landlords and property companies. Since 1919 virtually all the investment in new building has been undertaken either by local authorities for renting to families or by private developers for sale to owner-occupiers financed through the building societies. Many of the better quality terraced houses which have survived from the nineteenth century have also been sold by their landlords for owner occupation. The result, as already indicated in Tables 1.1 and 1.2, is that by 1976 more than eight in 10 households were either owner-occupiers or council tenants and that the majority of houses in those two sectors were relatively new.

The system of housing finance has had an equally important impact on the condition of the older houses which have survived the slum clearance programmes of the post-war period. When landlords have decided to sell for owner-occupation, the building societies which have provided the finance for the purchasers have typically restricted their lending to better quality houses in areas which are not threatened by planning blight or urban decay, and have also insisted on substantial works of repair or renovation as a condition of granting a mortgage. This means that older houses in the owner-occupied sector, which on average change hands about once every 10 years, are periodically subject to comprehensive repair and renovation. Quite apart from this house prices have risen rapidly. Owner-occupiers, who for the most part have higher than average incomes, have thus been required to spend relatively large amounts on good quality housing, though they receive substantial state assistance in the form of tax relief and improvement grants. Less well-off families who live in council houses have typically expected to pay less for their housing. But the system of subsidisation for the building and maintenance of council housing has meant that substantial sums of money have been contributed by central government and ratepayers towards the maintenance of relatively high standards in the council housing sector.

Neither of these systems of finance has, until recently, been readily available for the maintenance of standards in older houses in the private rented sector. Contrary to the general supposition there is no substantial difference in the treatment of owner-occupiers and private landlords in so far as tax relief on mortgage or interest payments is concerned. Private landlords are entitled to set interest payments off against their rental income before paying tax and are thus "subsidised" in a similar manner to owner-occupiers who are entitled to relief from taxation on interest payment on their mortgages. But until 1972 there was no state subsidy for lower income tenants in the private rented sector, and no official backing or approval for low interest loans over extended periods for the repair and renovation of privately rented houses. Furthermore under the Rent Acts the rents of small unfurnished houses and flats, below prescribed rateable values, were for a long period tied to the rents charged in 1913 or 1939, with limited permitted increases (see Andrew Arden, *Housing: Security and Rent Control*). This meant that the real income from rent controlled properties gradually declined and most landlords became increasingly reluctant to spend money on other than essential repairs. Many preferred to take the first opportunity, on the termination of a controlled tenancy, to sell their houses for owner occupation. The result was not only that new investment in houses and flats for renting at the lower end of the market dried up, but also that the condition of the existing privately rented houses progressively declined. The argument that this decline was due primarily to the profiteering instincts of private landlords as such rather than the cumulative effects of rent control is not entirely convincing. The condition of privately rented houses at the upper end of the uncontrolled sector is generally satisfactory, which indicates that landlords will generally maintain their properties provided that they are permitted to charge rents which will give them a reasonable return on their investment. The fact that there are continuing problems of repair and maintenance in regulated tenancies, in which due allowance for repairs is supposed to be made in the fixing of a fair rent, in areas of housing stress is better attributed to more general problems of urban decay than to the inherent deficiencies of private landlords. The figures in Table 1.2 indicate that local authorities find it as difficult as private landlords to maintain conditions in the older pre-1919 houses which they have acquired as a result of the progressive switch from slum clearance to rehabilitation. It has also been found in a recent survey that there are frequent complaints about the quality of the repairs service offered by local authorities in such older houses, flats and tenements, while tenants of modern council houses and flats are generally satisfied with repair and maintenance services (National

Consumer Council, *Do Council Tenants Get a Fair Deal on Repairs?* 1977).

3. *The Inner City Syndrome*

There are a number of more general factors which contribute to the general decline in housing conditions in inner city areas. Part of the problem is directly related to the trends in housing finance which have already been outlined. Access to owner-occupation is generally restricted to households which are relatively well off and thus eligible for building society mortgages. Access to council housing is generally restricted to well-established working class families who have themselves or through their parents a clear association with the area. And since most modern housing has been built in green field sites on the outskirts of cities and towns, many of the younger families eligible for mortgages or for council houses have in any event been removed from such inner city areas altogether. Those who remain are typically a mixture of older residents and pensioners and of more transient families and individuals, often immigrants from other parts of the country or abroad, who are not yet acceptable as council tenants and who have insufficient income to secure a mortgage.

These features of the housing market are simply a reflection of more general socio-economic forces. The relocation of many small businesses, factories and workshops from inner city to suburban sites and the decline of older staple industries has reduced employment opportunities in inner city areas. Those who have jobs are usually employed in low income service industries. New investment in employment and housing alike is often discouraged by planning blight resulting from the uncertainty as to the future of the areas, itself often caused by overambitious road schemes prepared by local authorities. All these problems combine to produce a vicious circle of low standards and expectations, and high levels of vandalism and decay.

These problems have a cumulative effect on all sectors of the housing market. As an area declines, better off families tend to move elsewhere, property values slump and building societies become more and more reluctant to grant mortgages on

houses in it. Council estates and tower blocks similarly suffer
from an exodus of higher income tenants, leaving a concentration of low income and "problem" families. But the inner
city syndrome is most readily observable in the private rented
sector, not least because it is often the only available source of
accommodation for those who make use of it. In areas where
there is already an established private rented sector, whether
of small single-household terrace houses or of flats and rooms
in larger three of four story houses, the principal effect is a
rapid deterioration in conditions. In other areas the owner-
occupiers gradually move out, and sell or rent their property.
Their place is typically taken by both absentee and resident
landlords, who subdivide the larger houses into a series of flats
or rooms with shared or inadequate facilities for cooking and
washing. Few of these landlords, except in some areas of
London, are established property companies, which prefer to
concentrate their activities at the top end of the private rented
sector. Most are individuals who have inherited properties they
do not wish to use, or bought properties for their own use but
cannot afford to use all the accommodation themselves. Some
may have borrowed at high rates of interest with a view to
providing accommodation for their own immigrant communities, and need to charge relatively high rents to meet the loan
repayments. The lack of other accommodation for those
excluded from council housing or owner occupation may itself
lead to overcrowding and a further deterioration in conditions.
In some cases landlords encourage overcrowding to increase
their profit, and put pressure on their tenants not to take legal
action either to secure an improvement in facilities or to
reduce excessive rents. In a few areas, scandalous and unlawful
practices develop, as highlighted in the report of the Milner
Holland Committee, *Housing in Greater London* (Cmnd. 2605,
1965). But the underlying cause of the abuses which occur in
such areas of housing stress is the exclusion of the people
concerned from the market for owner-occupied houses and the
failure of local councils to provide the kind of accommodation
which they require.

4. *Clearance, Rehabilitation or Renewal?*

Until the 1970s the main focus of official housing policy was on slum clearance and the building of new houses. Most local authorities had a rolling programme for the declaration of clearance areas, the rehousing of remaining occupants and the construction of new council housing on the site. The trouble with slum-clearance was that it usually took 10 to 15 years to get under way, that it blighted and eventually destroyed the inner city communities it was supposed to benefit and that it often produced only a new high rise concrete slum. As clearance programmes began to encroach on areas in which the houses were of better basic quality, local opposition to clearance increased and central government began to promote alternative policies of rehabilitation and renewal. Instead of large scale demolition and rebuilding, individual houses were to be rehabilitated with the assistance of government grants and renewal of the worst groups of houses was to be undertaken on a much more selective basis. Local authorities were given the power to declare improvement areas and later Housing Action Areas in which resources would be concentrated. Policies of this kind were intended to be less disruptive of established communities, to result in a more varied and sympathetic environment than many council estates and tower blocks and above all to be cheaper than large scale clearance and rebuilding.

These policies have also been linked with an attempt to build up a new co-operative housing sector. Voluntary housing associations may now be given substantial grants by the Housing Corporation to enable them to buy up older properties for rehabilitation and reletting. The development of housing associations may be supported both as a means of providing for people with special housing needs and as a contribution, along with municipalisation, to the elimination of the private landlord.

The merits of these various policies of clearance and rebuilding, of rehabilitation, and of the elimination of the private rented sector are a matter of current dispute. Policies of area renewal and rehabilitation have not turned out to be much cheaper than large scale clearance and redevelopment. And it has proved difficult to induce owners and landlords in the most run-down areas to co-operate in rehabilitating their own houses. These arguments are used by some to support a strategy of further municipalisation on the ground that satisfactory housing standards for lower income families and households can only be achieved by public bodies and that the elimination of the private rented sector should be pursued with all deliberate speed. Others claim that a substantial section of the population who for one reason or another do not wish to become owner-occupiers and who are not currently catered for adequately, or at all, by local authority housing, notably students and other young people in search of short term accommodation, will continue to depend on private landlords, and that policies should be developed to encourage private owners to continue to make such accommodation available provided that reasonable standards are maintained.

5. *Law and Policy*

These issues have not yet been resolved. Current policies provide the means both for an extension of municipalisation and for further support to the private rented sector through grants and loans. The point of this brief sketch of the nature of the housing problem and of the current policy debate is not to make a case for one particular strategy. It is to emphasise the extent to which law and policy are intertwined. The enforcement of the law by local authorities is likely to depend as much on the broader political objectives of central government and of individual local councils as on a direct legal interpretation of current legislation.

It is equally important to recognise the extent to which the existing law reflects the accumulation of a series of different policies which have been given legislative effect in successive statutes. This is especially the case in respect of the provisions for dealing with substandard and unfit housing under the Public Health and Housing Acts. These provisions have been built up in a piecemeal manner over the past century and have never been fully consolidated or rationalised in a coherent manner. It is therefore impossible to give a fully intelligible account of the law on compulsory repair and improvement without relating it to the development of housing policy and of the various administrative structures which that development has generated. The purpose of the next chapter is to explain the origin of the powers and duties imposed on local authorities under the Public Health and Housing Acts, and the way in which internal local government structures have been developed to administer them. Those who are primarily concerned with applying or giving advice on specific matters of current concern may wish to proceed immediately to Chapter 3.

Further Reading

General accounts of British housing policy may be found in J.B. Cullingworth, *Housing and Local Government* (1966), D.V. Donnison, *The Government of Housing* (1967), A. Murie, P. Niner and C. Watson, *Housing Policy and the Housing System* (1976), and D. Eversley, *The Politics of Housing* (1978).

The current official government view is given in the *Housing Policy Review* (Cmnd. 6851) (1977); the three Technical Volumes published in conjunction with the review provide a mass of historical and statistical information. Regular statistics are also published by the Department of the Environment in *Housing and Construction Statistics* and *Local Housing Statistics*.

2 The Development and Administration of Housing Law

Housing law is not a rationally thought out code. As with many other spheres of law, it is an accumulation of powers and procedures introduced at various periods to deal with particularly pressing problems. It is possible to give an account of the current interpretation and use of these various provisions without tracing their origin and development. But a full understanding of the current position and of the complex interaction of the Public Health and Housing Acts does require some historical knowledge. Such knowledge is all the more useful since the two codes of procedure have been developed and administered in separate departments within local authorities, each of which has built up its own traditions and attitudes. Environmental Health Departments, in succession to Public Health Departments, have been primarily concerned with the enforcement of the standards of health and hygiene prescribed in the Public Health Acts and have usually regarded the service of abatement notices in respect of housing disrepair in that wider context. Housing Departments have typically been concerned with the construction and management of council housing, and have until recently been involved with the private sector principally in the designation of areas of unfit housing with a view to clearance and redevelopment. These two traditions have been brought together in the past decade through the development of policies of improvement and rehabilitation in both the private and the public housing sectors. But the different backgrounds and approaches of officers trained in Public Health and Housing Departments are still observable, and sometimes cause strains within local authorities over the administration of housing programmes. The object of this chapter is to outline the separate development of the two codes of law and practice under the Public Health and Housing Acts, and to explain the way in which the functions of local authorities in this sphere are currently organised.

1. *The Public Health Acts*

The first concentrated attempt to control standards of housing was part of the more general campaign initiated by Edwin Chadwick in the early nineteenth century to improve standards of public hygiene. Before then legislation in this sphere, both national and local, had been limited to sporadic provisions to supplement the common law on the removal of nuisances — a polite name for the accumulation of the contents of privies and other household rubbish. In rural areas there was little general danger from poor hygiene. Infectious diseases and epidemics were regarded as part of the normal course of things, though the rural poor, who lived in very primitive conditions, were most at risk. State intervention was directed primarily at the relief of poverty and famine through the Poor Law rather than the improvement of housing conditions and sanitation. In urban areas there had been rather more attention to the provision of basic sewerage facilities in larger towns, and the more progressive corporations were already promoting local improvement statutes so that they might control the layout of new streets and regulate standards in new buildings.

As more and more workers began to flock into the new industrial towns in the eighteenth and nineteenth centuries the problems of public health and hygiene became much more pressing. Sanitary facilities in the houses in terraces and courts provided by factory owners and their associates for the new class of factory workers were virtually non-existent. There was often little ventilation, not least due to the practice of building houses back to back or in enclosed courts. The dangers of epidemics were greatly increased by gross overcrowding in some districts, with whole families living in single rooms or cellars or in communal lodging houses.

The initial pressure to control these abuses was a mixture of the growth of medical science on the causes of epidemics, and of philanthropy and self-protection on the part of the business and professional classes. Increased powers to deal with sewerage, water supply, the removal of nuisances and the control of infectious diseases and to regulate new building were provided piecemeal for a whole range of local bodies from the established town corporations, parish vestries and poor law boards to newly constituted sewerage boards, water commissioners, and nuisance removal authorities and committees. Many of these provisions originated in local statutes promoted by individual town corporations, as for instance in the Liverpool Act of 1842. They were first consolidated in the Town Improvement Clauses Act 1847 and the Public Health Act 1848. Most of these newly generalised powers, however, were permissive rather than compulsory. Though most of the larger towns did appoint public health officers and did seek to enforce some control over new building, some did not. The widespread opposition to any extension in central government power prevented any effective supervision or enforcement by the newly constituted Board of Health in London, set up under the statute of 1848. Further problems were created by the chaotic allocation of the various powers and duties among the various local bodies and committees.

This pattern of piecemeal legislation initiated by progressive local authorities in private statutes and subsequently generalised for the use of all authorities has continued to be a feature of the development of the law in this sphere and accounts for some of the complexity of the system. For present purposes it is sufficient to focus attention on those aspects of the law which have survived till the present, notably the concept of a statutory nuisance and the regulation of new building.

The established common law conception of nuisance was first given a statutory definition — "any dwelling house in such a filthy and unwholesome condition as to be a nuisance to or injurious to the health of any person" — in the Nuisance Removal Act of 1848, introduced as a temporary measure to deal with a serious cholera epidemic. The powers granted to local nuisance removal authorities, which might be constituted by town corporations, local boards, improvement commissioners, poor law guardians or specially created nuisance removal committees, to bring persons causing nuisances before the local magistrates and where necessary to remove the nuisance themselves, were then consolidated and made permanent in the Nuisance Removal Acts of 1855 and 1860. Further extensions in the coverage of these provisions and in the system of enforcement were made under the leadership of Sir John Simon in the Sanitary Act 1866: the concept of a statutory nuisance was extended to cover simple overcrowding, in rented houses and public lodging houses alike, as well as physical conditions and accumulations; powers to permit local police and central government to initiate proceedings where the nuisance removal authority failed to act were also inserted. Then under the Local Government Act 1871 the responsibilities and powers of all the various local bodies and committees were at last brought together in a single local government board for each district. Under the Public Health Act of the following year the provisions relating to public health were further extended and consolidated.

These provisions were finally reenacted in the great Public Health Act of 1875, which remained in force until 1936 and which still dominates the basic form of public health legislation. The standard enforcement procedures, however, involving the service of formal abatement notices backed up by quasi-criminal proceedings in local magistrates courts and by powers for the local authority to act in default, may be traced back to the old nuisance removal statutes. The right of individuals to go straight to the local magistrates court to secure action, discussed in detail in Chapter 4, is likewise derived from the procedure designed by Sir John Simon to permit local activists to force dilatory local authorities to use their powers. The definition of a statutory nuisance and the statutory list of items covered also reflect the preoccupations of the mid-nineteenth century: "any pool, ditch, gutter, watercourse, privy, urinal so foul as to be a nuisance or injurious to health; any accumulation or deposit which is a nuisance or injurious to health ... " and so on. The effective scope of the most general phrase, "any premises in such a state as to be a nuisance or injurious to health," however, has been progressively extended as standards and expectations have risen from matters of sanitation and ventilation to cover virtually any form of disrepair which may affect occupiers. It is now widely used to deal with loose slates, rotting floors and other relatively minor defects as well as blocked or defective drains and sewers (see Chapter 4).

The process of extension in public health legislation has also followed the established nineteenth century pattern. More progressive local authorities have continued to promote local statutes to obtain special powers to deal more effectively with specific problems such as vermin and blocked drains. The more standard clauses have then been inserted in general statutes, as for instance in the supplementation of the standard enforcement procedures laid down in the Public Health Act 1936 by the expedited procedures in the Public Health Act 1961.

The primary concern of public health departments, or environmental health departments as they are now called, is not with housing conditions as such but with the general protection of the public in matter of health and hygiene. Most of the time of public health officers is devoted to the inspection of food processing and preparation, slaughter houses and other such matters. Many of their specific powers in relation to housing conditions, however, notably the enforcement of the Building Regulations and the administration of compulsory repair and improvement notices, have been increasingly separated from the main stream of public health work. Before the current allocation of responsibility in these matters within local authorities can be adequately explained, the development of the second limb of housing legislation must also be described.

2. *Housing for the Working Classes*

It was obvious to the reformers of the nineteenth century that it was just as important to encourage and require better standards in the building of new houses as to deal with public health risks in existing slums. During the early part of the century some of the more humane and philanthropic factory owners were already making provision for relatively good quality terrace houses for their workers, as for instance in the various factory settlements organised by Robert Owen. Others showed their concern at the appalling conditions in the worst industrial towns by arranging public subscriptions for the construction of model terraces or courts. The more progressive town corporations, as has been seen, were also beginning to regulate the layout of new streets and the standards of new building through local improvement statutes. As with other such measures these powers were eventually generalised in subsequent Public Health Acts. They are currently provided for under the Public Health Act 1961 and known collectively as the Building Regulations. They are usually enforced by a separate body of building inspectors attached to the City Engineer's or Surveyor's Department.

Wider powers than were available for the abatement of nuisances were also developed to deal with individual unfit houses, and then with whole areas of unsanitary or unfit houses. Under the Artisans and Labourers Dwellings Act 1868 local authorities were given a power to require the owners of houses considered to be "in a condition or state dangerous to health so as to be unfit for human habitation" either to carry out specified works or else to demolish the houses. And under the Artisans and Labourers Dwellings Improvement Act 1875 local authorities were granted powers to require the demolition of "unhealthy areas" in which the "houses, courts or alleys ... were unfit for human habitation" or in which ill health was prevalent due to "the closeness, narrowness and bad arrangement or the bad condition of the streets and houses ... or to the want of light, air, or proper conveniences," with a view to encouraging a scheme of improvement. Then under the Housing of the Working Classes Act 1885 a general provision was introduced that houses let to members of the working classes should at the start of any tenancy be "in all respects fit for human habitation." Frequent amendments were made to these provisions in subsequent statutes and in the major consolidations in the Housing of the Working Classes Act 1890 and the Housing Act 1930. But most of the basic rules and procedural requirements in respect of individual unfit houses and of slum clearance programmes, discussed in detail in Chapters 4 and 8, may be traced back to these initial statutes.

Throughout the nineteenth century, however, it was considered to be inappropriate for local authorities themselves to provide the housing needed to accommodate those displaced by clearance or demolition. The schemes of improvement provided for in early housing statutes were intended to be carried out by private landlords. The first general statute in this sphere, the Labouring Classes Dwellings Act 1866, was designed to provide central government finance for this purpose, and any new building by local authorities was strictly controlled. Under the Artisans and Labourers Dwellings Improvement Act 1875 specific authority from central government was required before any local authority might itself embark on an improvement scheme, and under the Housing for the Working Classes Act 1890 local authorities which did build new houses were required to dispose of them within 10 years. Despite these restrictive provisions a few authorities, notably in London, Liverpool and Sheffield, did provide substantial numbers of houses and flats for permanent letting. But the bulk of the new housing for working class families was provided by private landlords, supplemented in some areas by low rent non-profit making developments by charitable bodies like the Peabody Trust in London. By the end of the war of 1914-1918 the total number of council houses was reckoned to be a mere 20,000, compared with a total figure of almost five million houses constructed between 1871 and 1918.

3.   *The Growth of Owner-Occupation and Council Housing*

In the aftermath of the war of 1914-1918 there was a radical change of approach in housing policy. It was at last recognised that substantial progress in slum clearance and new house building alike required some form of subsidy, since members of the working classes could not afford to pay the full cost of better quality housing. It has been calculated that in 1907 the economic rent of a new terrace house which complied with current building regulations was some five to six shillings a week, which amounted to about 18 per cent of the average earnings per week of a manual worker (*Housing Policy Review*, Technical Volume I, Ch. 1, para. 8). This was too much for many families, and house building fell off sharply in the immediate pre-war period. The rigid controls on the rents of cheaper privately rented houses and flats introduced during the war and made permanent under the Rent Acts from 1920 onwards (see Andrew Arden, *Housing: Security and Rent Control*, Ch. 1) exacerbated the problem. Eventually in the

Housing (Additional Powers) Act 1919 a central government subsidy for newly built houses was introduced. This could take the form either of a lump sum capital payment, initially fixed at £75 per house, which represented about one third of the total building cost of a minimum standard dwelling, or else a continuing annual subsidy, initially fixed at £6 per annum over a 20 year period. This system was extended under the Housing Act 1923, and remained in force, though with frequent changes in the extent and amount of the subsidy, until 1967.

The effect of the twin policies of rent control and subsidised building was the very rapid increase in owner occupation and in council housing which has already been referred to in Chapter 1.

The increase in owner occupation was not due entirely to the offer of state subsidy on smaller houses. An equally important factor was the steady expansion in the 1920s and 1930s of the building society movement through which most of the speculative suburban building of the period was ultimately financed. The conversion of the major building societies from essentially local cooperative savings societies into national financial institutions prepared to lend money to any applicant who could establish an ability to meet the necessary mortgage repayments greatly increased the class of people who could afford to become owner occupiers. This in turn greatly enlarged the market not only for newly built subsidised houses but also for existing houses which many landlords were now anxious to sell for owner-occupation. As the figures in Table 2.1 show, almost half the net increase in owner-occupation in the period from 1914 to 1960 was the result of transfers from the private rented sector.

The increase in council housing was due primarily to a change in political attitudes. The growth of the Labour Party at national and local levels finally disposed of the prevailing nineteenth century idea that it was inappropriate for state bodies to become involved in the provision of housing. Some Labour controlled councils were prepared to give a further subsidy to their tenants in addition to that provided by central government by running their housing accounts at a loss and making up the balance by a transfer from rating revenue. An

Table 2.1
Changes in Patterns of Tenure as a Result of New Building,
Transfers and Slum-Clearance, England and Wales 1914-1975

	Owner-occupation (000s)		Council Housing (000s)		Privately Rented (000s)	
Position in 1914	800	(9%)	20	(*%)	7,900	(91%)
Changes 1914-1938						
New building	+1,800		+1,100		+ 900	
Transfers	+1,100		-		-1,100	
Slum-clearance	-		-		-300	
Position in 1938	3,700	(32%)	1,100	(10%)	6,600	(58%)
Changes 1939-1960						
New building	+1,300		+2,300		+ 100	
Transfers	+1,500		+200		-1,700	
Slum-clearance	-100		-		-400	
Position in 1960	6,400	(44%)	3,600	(25%)	4,600	(32%)
Changes 1961-1975						
New building	+2,600		+1,600		+ 300	
Transfers	+1,100		+100		-1,200	
Slum-clearance	-200		-100		-800	
Position in 1975	9,900	(55%)	5,200	(29%)	2,900	(16%)

Source: *Housing Policy Review*, Technical Volume I, Tables 1.23-24

equally important factor was the development of slum clearance programmes. Both in the 1930s and from about 1950 onwards a major focus of local authority housing activity in urban areas was the designation of clearance areas and the construction of new council estates both on the cleared sites and also in newly acquired "green field" sites in the suburbs. Local authorities were required by the Housing Acts to give a formal undertaking that suitable alternative accommodation would be available for those displaced by clearance programmes before ministerial consent was given, and since it often took many years for inner city sites to be cleared and redeveloped, many of those affected had to be rehoused elsewhere. In the period from 1914 until 1975 almost two million houses were demolished, the large majority from the private rented sector. The number of council houses built in the same period, however, was far in excess of the houses required to provide for those displaced, particularly in the 1950s. Though council housing has not played as significant a role in the decline of the private rented sector as the switch to owner-occupation, it has in the last decade become the major alternative to owner-occupation.

The pursuit of slum clearance programmes, like all large scale bureaucratic exercises, generated its own problems. In many areas there was a tendency for huge areas of older housing in inner city areas to be designated as clearance or potential clearance areas long before there was any realistic prospect of action on the ground. The planning blight which this caused and the resulting exclusion of building society finance helped to accelerate the deterioration in housing standards in such twilight areas. The result was a progressive increase in opposition to large scale clearance. Further impetus to the search for more acceptable alternatives was given by the encroachment of clearance schemes on areas of relatively good quality housing and by the fact that some newly built housing estates and tower blocks were proving almost as unsatisfactory in terms of repairs and a good deal less attractive in terms of living environment than the terrace housing which they replaced. By the late 1960s these pressures were strong enough to cause a major shift in policy from clearance to rehabilitation.

4. *Legislation for Rehabilitation*

Legislation for rehabilitation rather than clearance and rebuilding dates back to the earliest housing statutes. Under the Artisans and Labourers Dwellings Act 1868, as has been seen, local authorities were given power to require owners to improve unsanitary houses rather than demolish them. These powers were refined and extended in subsequent Housing Acts. Under the Housing Act 1957 local authorities may still require owners to render unfit houses fit, provided that the necessary works can be carried out at reasonable expense, and a further power to require the repair of houses which were not unfit but in substantial disrepair was added in 1969 (see Chapter 4). Until recently, however, these powers have not been widely used. The most significant governmental contribution to rehabilitation has been the provision of grants for the installation of standard amenities and for more general improvements.

The initial legislation for grants in 1949 was limited to the provision of bathrooms and other standard amenities in houses which lacked them. Since then the scope of grants has been progressively extended. In 1959 provision was made for discretionary grants for the rehabilitation of smaller houses or the conversion of larger houses into a number of flats or maisonettes. In 1969 the level of grants was substantially increased. And under the Housing Act 1974 provision was added for grants for repairs only in certain limited cases. In each case, however, the basic pattern established in 1949 has been followed, in that those who apply for grants are given only a proportion of the total expenditure and must undertake to meet local authority requirements in respect of the standards of work to be done (see Chapter 5).

These measures proved relatively successful. In the period from 1949 to 1976 more than two million houses in England and Wales were provided with bathrooms and other amenities with standard amenity grants; from 1959 to 1976 a total of more than 1,600,000 discretionary improvement and conversion grants were also approved. The greatest impact, however, was made in relatively good quality housing, by established owner-occupiers, by those buying houses with the assistance of building society mortgages and by local authorities themselves. Many fewer grants were taken up in run-down inner city areas, where owner-occupiers and landlords alike found it difficult or uneconomic to raise their contribution to schemes of improvement. The response of central government was to encourage local authorities to adopt an area approach to improvement, following the pattern which was already familiar for clearance and redevelopment. In 1964 provision was made for the declaration of Improvement Areas, later to be known as General Improvement Areas (GIAs), in which local authorities are intended both to encourage owners to take up grants and to contribute to the general improvement of facilities by providing such things as play areas and open spaces. Then in 1974 provision was made for the declaration of Housing Action Areas (HAAs) in which local authorities are expected to play a much more active role, both in inducing private owners to take up grants, which may be paid at much higher levels, and in acquiring and improving houses themselves, if necessary by the use of compulsory purchase powers.

It is too early to make any final assessment of the merits of the switch from clearance to rehabilitation, or of the efficacy of the area approach. The details of the law and its administration and of the progress which has been made and the problems which have been encountered will be given in Chapter 7. For present purposes it is sufficient to focus attention on the impact of rehabilitation programmes on the internal organisation of local authorities. In most areas a separate and relatively independent section within the Housing or Environmental Health Department has been created to deal with grant applications and the supervision of grant aided works. The development of programmes of area rehabilitation, however, required a more integrated approach, since functions usually carried out by a number of different departments were involved. Central government recommended the setting up of interdepartmental teams with representatives from Housing and Environmental Health Departments and other departments as appropriate. This advice has been followed in many areas, with the result that additional sections or teams have been created with such titles as "Urban Renewal Team" or "Housing Action Area Team." The processing of grant applications, the clearing of plans for compliance with the Building Regulations and other such matters, however, have usually been left under the control of existing departments or sections.

5. *Local Authority Organisation*

The result of these various statutory and policy developments is that responsibility for housing in general and for rehabilitation programmes in particular is frequently split between a number of distinct departments and sections within local authorities. The major role is usually played by Housing and Environmental Health Departments, but there is also substantial involvement by Estates, Planning, Architect's or Surveyor's and Finance or Treasurer's Departments. There is no regular pattern in these matters, since local authorities are left to create their own internal structures. But it may be helpful to give a brief sketch of the functions which are usually carried out by each department, if only to assist those individuals who find the multiplicity of departments and sections with which they may have to deal somewhat confusing.

The principal function of Housing Departments is the management and allocation of council housing. Maintenance and repair of council houses and flats is usually the responsibility of a separate section within the department, which may or may not employ its own direct labour force for this purpose. The preparation and administration of schemes for slum clearance and redevelopment is also dealt with by a separate section in many authorities. Responsibility for the selection, purchase and rehabilitation of older houses in HAAs, GIAs and elsewhere for use by the council has sometimes been allocated to these established clearance and redevelopment sections; but in some areas new sections within the Housing Department or on an interdepartmental basis have been established for this purpose. In some areas the administration of grants is also allocated to the Housing Department.

The principal function of the Environmental Health Department is the enforcement of the provisions of the Public Health Acts and related legislation like the Clean Air Acts. Much of this work has nothing to do with housing, and involves the inspection of cafes, restaurants, abatoirs, and other forms of food processing as well as the supervision of the sanitation system and the control of infectious diseases. But public health inspectors have traditionally been responsible for the inspection of houses with a view to classifying them as fit or unfit for the purpose of slum clearance and redevelopment programmes. They are also responsible in most areas for the service and enforcement of compulsory repair and improvement notices under the Public Health and Housing Acts (see Chapter 4). In some areas they are also responsible for the administration of grants. The administration of the Building

Regulations, however, is usually the responsibility of a separate section within the Surveyor's or Engineer's Department, despite the fact that they are formally enacted under the Public Health Acts.

A number of other departments are less directly involved in housing as such, but may have to be dealt with by those involved in schemes for rehabilitation or renewal. The Planning Department is naturally concerned with all schemes which constitute development within the Town and Country Planning Acts or which affect the long term future of individual houses or areas, and may have to give approval for any grant application which requires the house in question to have an expected future life of any given number of years. The Estates Department will usually be responsible for any purchase of property by the local authority, whether voluntarily or by the use of compulsory purchase powers, and thus for any negotiation on the price to be paid. The Finance or Treasurer's Department will usually be responsible for considering applications for loans and mortgages for house purchase or rehabilitation. And the Solicitor's Department or Town Clerk's Department may well be involved in any matter which is likely to result in other than routine legal proceedings.

It will be clear even from this brief account that local authorities are highly complex organisations, and that what may appear to the outsider to be relatively straightforward matters may require the attention of several different departments. In theory the local authority is a single corporate body which acts under the authority of its elected councillors. In practice it is made up of a large number of distinct bureaucracies, each with its own traditions and attitudes. Those who can find the time to unravel the way in which their own local authority is organised and to approach the correct department or section in respect of each relevant issue will make much more rapid and less frustrating progress than those who assume that each officer and department represents a single rational body.

Further Reading

A detailed account of the development of public health and housing legislation may be found in R. Lambert, *Sir John Simon and English Social Administration* (1963); general accounts may be found in any good social history of the nineteenth century. The best sources for an understanding of contemporary concerns are Chadwick's *Report on the sanitary condition of the labouring population of Great Britain* (1842) and the *First and Second Reports of the Royal Sanitary Commission* (1868-69 and 1871); useful details may also be found in A.P. Stewart and E. Jenkins, *The Medical and Legal Aspects of Sanitary Reform* (1866), republished with an introduction by M.W. Flinn in 1969.

3 Responsibility for Maintenance and Repair and the Enforcement of Tenancy Agreements

It is vital in any discussion of legal duties on maintenance and repair to distinguish the various classes of tenure: owner-occupiers, tenants, licensees and trespassers. The precise nature of these classes has been explained at length in the companion to this volume (Andrew Arden, *Housing: Security and Rent Control*, ch. 2). Fortunately the nature of the tenure is unlikely to cause difficulties in most cases. The basic legal rules are quite straightforward. In the case of owner-occupiers, whether under a mortgage or as outright owners, the natural legal assumption is that the owner is responsible for all aspects of the maintenance, repair and improvement of his house. For other forms of tenure the natural legal assumption is that it is up to the parties, the owner of the house and its occupants, to make what arrangements they please on these matters. There may be what is called a "full repairing" lease, tenancy or license under which the occupier has undertaken to be responsible for all maintenance and repairs. Or there may be a more complex allocation of duties between the parties. Under any form of lease, tenancy or license it is therefore essential to begin by looking at the precise terms of the agreement. Any party to it may then seek to enforce its provisions by action in the courts. In the case of trespassers there can be no contractual obligations on either side.

These rules are not always sufficient to fix responsibility when problems arise. The main difficulty with the contractual approach for rented houses is that there is often no precise provision in respect of the particular defect which may appear, or indeed any formal agreement at all, either written or oral. In such cases the courts have to decide what terms can reasonably be implied in the absence of express agreement. The courts have also to decide in respect of all premises on the

extent of owners' and occupiers' liability to people who are not
parties to any express or implied agreement, for instance
visitors who fall down defective staircases or who are injured by
falling slates. In addition Parliament has intervened to impose
certain basic duties on owners and landlords, irrespective of
contract, in respect of houses and flats let at low rents or on
short term or continuing tenancies.

This chapter begins with a discussion of the statutory terms
prescribed in the Housing Acts and of the common law rules
on express and implied covenants which govern those cases
which do not fall under the statutory provisions. This is
followed by an explanation of how these various terms and
covenants may be enforced by action in the courts or by "self-
help" methods. The separate rules in respect of liability for
injuries arising from failure to maintain or repair will then be
set out.

1. *The Provisions of Tenancy Agreements*

Statutory terms

The most important practical consideration in most tenancies is the statutory covenant implied under the Housing Act
1961, s. 32. This imposes on all landlords in respect of all
tenancies of less than seven years granted since October 1,
1961 the following obligations, regardless of the formal
provisions of the tenancy agreement:

  (a) to keep in repair the structure and exterior of the
      dwelling-house (including drains, gutters and exter-
      nal pipes); and
  (b) to keep in repair and proper working order the
      installations in the dwelling-house
      (i) for the supply of water, gas and electricity, and
          for sanitation (including basins, sinks, baths and
          sanitary conveniences but not ... fixtures, fittings
          and appliances for making use of the supply of
          water, gas and electricity), and
      (ii) for space heating or heating water.

Both council tenants and private sector tenants are accordingly protected. But it should be noted that while a continuing

weekly or monthly tenancy is clearly a tenancy of less than
seven years, it may nonetheless be excluded if it was initially
granted before 1961. The only way in which these obligations
can be avoided by the landlord is by a formal application to
the county court which may if it thinks it reasonable in all the
circumstances and if both landlord and tenant agree authorise
an agreement to vary the statutory covenants (s. 32(6)). This is
rarely done.

The precise application of these statutory terms should not
give much difficulty. The standard of repair required is
expressly stated to be what is reasonable in relation to the age,
character and prospective life of the house and the area in
which it is situated. "Structure and exterior" clearly includes
such matters as ceilings, staircases, windows, roofing, and
pointing. It does not include decoration, either internal or
external, nor the replacement of items such as windows broken
by the tenant or his family or visitors. There is some dispute
over outside paths, passages, yards and fences. It has been held
by the courts that a short concrete path and steps leading to a
public pavement is included (*Brown* v. *Liverpool Corporation*
(1969)); but it has also been held that a back-yard giving
access to an alleyway is not included (*Hopwood* v. *Cannock
Chase District Council* (1975)). The rule in such cases appears
to be that the principal means of access to the house or flat is
part of the exterior, but that yards, gardens and fences are
not. In cases of doubt the issue must in the end be decided by
the courts.

Brief mention should also be made of the additional statutory covenant incorporated in certain tenancies under the
Housing Act 1957, s. 6. This imposes on landlords an obligation to ensure that the house is fit for human habitation at the
start of the tenancy and is maintained in that state throughout. But the section applies only to houses let at very low rents:
on contracts made after 1957 at an annual rent (including
rates) of not more than £52 (in London £80); on contracts
made before 1957 in towns of more than 50,000 at less than £26
(in London £40); and on contracts in smaller towns made
between 1923 and 1957 at less than £26 or before 1923 at less
than £16. Since council tenancies and those on houses regulated
under the Rent Acts are almost certain to exceed these limits the

effective application of this provision is to houses whose rents have long been *controlled* under the Rent Acts, and few even of those currently fall within the statutory limits. For this reason a discussion of the precise meaning of fitness for human habitation will be postponed until the next chapter, where the much more generally applicable rules in relation to the repair of unfit houses are discussed. For present purposes it is suffi- cient to state that there will be few if any cases in which the protection given under the Housing Act 1957 is not effectively replaced and increased under the Housing Act 1961.

There are certain more general and significant limitations on these statutory covenants which arise from the way in which the sections are formulated. In each case the effect of the legis- lation is to incorporate the statutory covenants in the tenancy which already exists, whether it is in writing or not, between a landlord and his tenant. This means that only those who are entitled to the formal legal status of tenant can rely on or enforce the covenants. Those who occupy a house under a licence (see Andrew Arden, *Housing: Security and Rent Control*) are not protected; nor of course are those who are trespassers. Any action to enforce the landlord's duty must be initiated by the person who is legally regarded as the tenant. This should cause little practical difficulty, since if there is a tenancy at all, there must be a tenant and all that is required is his or her consent to whatever action is contemplated. For instance if the original tenant of a council house dies or moves, any successor who is accepted as a tenant and is given a rent book will automatically become entitled to rely on the statu- tory covenants.

The second major limitation is the requirement that notice must be given to the landlord of the need for repair before the covenants can be enforced or relied on. This rule was estab- lished in a series of personal injury cases, and applies both to obvious and concealed or latent defects:

O'Brien v. Robinson (1973)
The ceiling of a flat fell on the tenant and his wife and injured them. Three years previously they had com- plained about prolonged dancing and banging in the flat above, but no observable damage had been caused to the ceiling then or since. It was held that since no notice had

been given, or could have been given, to the landlord of the defective state of the ceiling, there could be no liability to repair under the terms of the Housing Act 1961, s. 32; nor could the landlord be held liable for injury resulting from such a latent defect of which he had neither knowledge nor notice.

These decisions have been criticised as an illegitimate and unnecessary judicial curtailment of the intention of Parliament to make the landlord absolutely responsible for such defects. But in so far as actions to require the landlord to remedy defects, as opposed to actions for personal injury or damage, are concerned the rule is not unreasonable.

A third general limitation is sometimes raised in respect of the reasonableness of the cost of any repairs required under the statutory covenants. This supposed limitation arises from a decision that a landlord may not be held responsible for breach of the statutory covenant to keep the premises fit for human habitation where the cost of the repairs would be unreasonable, since there is a concurrent statutory obligation on local authorities to require the owners of houses which cannot be made fit at reasonable expense to demolish them or close them until they have been made fit (see Chapter 4):

Buswell v. Goodwin (1971)

The landlord bought a house with a sitting tenant, and agreed to make the premises fit in return for an increase in rent. No repairs were done. Some years later the local authority served a closing order on the landlord on the ground that the house was unfit and could not be made fit at reasonable expense. The landlord claimed possession on the ground that the statutory tenancy had been terminated by the closing order. The tenant claimed that the landlord was in breach of his statutory duty under the Housing Act 1957, s. 6 to keep the premises fit and could not rely on his own failure to do so. It was held that the covenant under section 6 did not apply to a house which could not be made fit at reasonable expense; nor was the landlord in breach of any express agreement since no contract on the rent to be paid when the house had been repaired had been concluded.

This decision has also been widely criticised. But it is clear from the brief summary of the case that no such limitation can be raised in respect of the statutory covenant under the Housing Act 1961, unless the failure to repair is sufficiently serious to render the house unfit. Since as already explained the statutory covenants under the Housing Act 1961 effectively replace and extend those under the Housing Act 1957, the reasonable expense limitation can usually be safely ignored.

The common law on repairs: freedom of contract

Where for one reason or another the statutory covenants cannot be relied on, it is necessary to revert to the old common law rules on the relations between landlord and tenant. The foundation on which these rules are based is the concept of freedom of contract. The landlord and his tenants or licensees are supposed to be in an equal bargaining position and thus to be able to allocate their various rights and duties, in respect of rent and security of tenure as well as of repairs, on a fair basis. The old legal maxim was that "there is no law against letting a tumbledown house." As with the statutory covenants, there is no formal distinction in this respect between the private rented sector and local authority housing, or between tenants and licensees. The parties to all such contracts are regarded as being free to make any agreement they please, subject only to whatever statutory provisions may apply.

The reality is rather different. Large landlords in practice draw up their own standard form tenancy agreements, or get their solicitors to do it for them. The clauses are usually taken from established legal precedent books in which the same old phrases are copied and preserved from generation to generation. In most cases the draftsman seeks to make the tenant responsible for everything. A typical repairs clause, taken from the Belfast Corporation tenancy used until 1972, might read as follows:

> The Tenant shall keep the interior of the premises hereby let clean and in good tenantable repair and condition ...
> If any part of the said premises or the fittings therein are damaged by the Tenant, or through his negligence ... , the Corporation shall be at liberty to enter on the said premises and repair and cleanse the same at the cost of

the Tenant, who shall repay on demand to the Corporation the cost of such repairs and/or cleansing as certified by the Estates Superintendent. The Tenant shall immediately replace any cracked or broken glass belonging to the said premises, and at least once in every twelve months cause all chimneys in use to be properly swept.

In dealing with clauses of this kind it is always important to study the precise words used carefully and critically. The example which has been given, it should be noted, could not be enforced in England and Wales in a tenancy granted since 1961. Nor is it as harsh as may appear at first sight. A second reading shows that the tenant is required to maintain only the *interior* of the premises, so that any disrepair to the exterior and perhaps even to the structure may remain the responsibility of the landlord. The difficulty is that tenancy agreements rarely state what the landlord is obliged to do. Local authorities in their capacity as landlords are as cautious in this respect as private landlords: a recent study of a sample of 318 council tenancy agreements showed that three-quarters did not contain *any clause* imposing *any duty* on the local authority, though almost all contained a whole series of clauses imposing obligations and restrictions on tenants (National Consumer Council, *Tenancy agreements between councils and their tenants* (1976)). It cannot be assumed, as will be seen, that what is not imposed as an obligation on the tenant is therefore accepted as an obligation by the landlord.

Implied terms

The courts have over the years built up a series of rules to deal with the allocation of responsibilities when there is no express provision in the tenancy. During the nineteenth century it became established law that in the absence of express terms to the contrary the landlord of furnished premises was bound to maintain the premises in a fit state for occupation. This rule, it should be noted, was not derived from any great concern on the part of the judges to promote better conditions but to allow tenants who had contracted for a given period to leave without further payment:

Smith v. *Marrable* (*1843*)
Sir Thomas and Lady Marrable rented a furnished house
in Brighton for a period of five weeks. On arrival they
found it infested with bugs, and left a few days later. The
landlord sued for the balance of the rent due for the five
week period. The suit was rejected on the ground that any
person who lets a ready-furnished house does so under an
implied condition that the house is in a fit state to be
inhabited.

The rule has nonetheless become settled law and may still be
relied upon.

It has also been established that in the absence of any
express term the landlord of a block of flats or group of houses
will be held responsible for the maintenance and repair of any
common parts which are not included in any specific tenancy.
The landlord is thus responsible for the due upkeep of things
like hallways, stairs, passages and lifts which are used by
tenants generally. But this obligation is not absolute. The
landlord, whether private or public, is not required to do more
than can be reasonably expected, and will not necessarily be
liable for a failure to maintain facilities if the immediate cause
is vandalism or other external intervention:

Liverpool City Council v. *Irwin* (*1976*)
The tenants of a tower block of flats went on rent strike
on the ground that the council was failing to repair and
maintain the lifts, rubbish chutes, stairs and passages.
The council sought possession of the tenants' flats on the
ground of failure to pay rent. The tenancy agreement
made no reference to any duty on the part of the council
to maintain the common parts. It was held in the House
of Lords that the landlord of a block of flats must maintain the means of access to individual flats, unless the
obligation to do so is placed in a defined manner on the
tenants individually or collectively; but that the landlord
is entitled to expect the tenants to act reasonably; since
the council had repeatedly repaired the lifts and chutes
in response to repeated vandalism, there had not been any
breach of the implied term.

The courts have been equally cautious in developing other
implied terms. In the nineteenth century the judges repeatedly

refused to extend to unfurnished premises the implied duty to keep furnished premises in a fit state for occupation on the ground that it would be an unwarrantable interference in the freedom of landlords and tenants to make their own contracts. This view prevailed until Parliament intervened through the Housing of the Working Classes Act 1885 to impose on landlords of all houses for letting to members of the working class a condition that at the commencement of the tenancy the house should be in all respects fit for human habitation (see Chapter 2). More recently some judges have adopted a less restrictive approach. In one case arising out of an injury to a passer-by from the collapse of a wall, Lord Denning suggested that in all weekly or monthly continuing tenancies in which the landlord expressly or impliedly reserved a right of entry to inspect the premises, he should also be regarded as responsible for any defects of which he knew or should have known (*Mint* v. *Good* (1951)). And in a subsequent case Lord Justice Willmer suggested that where a tenant was obliged to reside in a council flat in order to retain his tenancy, an obligation on the council to keep the flat fit for human habitation might be implied; but the court decided that in the absence of an express term or a statutory obligation no *general* obligation on the council to carry out minor repairs could be implied, even where it regularly carried out such repairs on request from tenants:

Sleafer v. *Lambeth Borough Council (1960)*
The standard form tenancy of the Lambeth Borough Council prohibited tenants from carrying out any repair work without permission, and the council regularly did all the repairs and maintenance which it considered necessary. The tenant of a flat, who had done some decoration to his front door without permission, complained that the door was sticking. Shortly after he was injured when the handle fell off as he was attempting to close it. He sued the council for damages for breach of an alleged implied term to maintain the premises in good repair. The action was dismissed: the Court of Appeal upheld the view of the trial judge that while the tenants were aware that the council did in fact carry out repairs, that amounted to no more than an expectation or hope; the council had carefully avoided binding themselves to do any repairs in the formal contract, and no such term could be implied.

It is arguable that this decision would not now be followed, and that tenants may rely on established practice as a ground for implying a legal obligation to carry out repairs, on the ground that landlords who carry out repairs on request are prevented or estopped from subsequently denying any obligation to do so. But there is as yet no clear judicial authority for the extension of the established doctrine of equitable estoppel to the field of landlord and tenant.

It is clear from this brief discussion that the law on implied terms is unsatisfactory and uncertain. In the first place the courts have no power to overrule the express terms of any contract unless they are clearly self-contradictory or unworkable. The first step in ascertaining the rights and duties of landlords and tenants must always be a careful and detailed reading of the whole of the tenancy agreement. In cases where there is no relevant provision, some assistance may be given by the courts. But the circumstances in which a formal legal duty will be imposed on landlords are strictly limited. More progress is likely to be made in this field by the development of statutory covenants which may not be excluded by any express provisions than by test cases designed to extend the current range of readily implied terms. The Law Commission has already recommended the extension of the provisions of the Housing Acts 1957 and 1961 to cover the duty of landlords to maintain common parts (Report No. 67, *Obligations of Landlords and Tenants*, 1975).

More progress is likely to be made by requiring local authorities to draw up fairer and more comprehensive tenancy agreements. The Housing Bill published in March 1979 by the Labour Government provided, as part of its Tenants Charter, that local authorities should publish straightforward summaries both of their tenancy agreements and of their housing allocation schemes. But that is not enough. Local authority tenancy agreements should also be required to meet certain minimum standards of clarity and fairness, and should be subject to review by an independent body. The National Consumer Council has provided a useful model agreement, setting out in detail the obligations of the council and the rights of tenants over different types of repairs (*Tenancy Agreements between Councils and their Tenants*, 1976). But precise terms should not be prescribed, so that tenants associations in particular streets or estates may make special agreements, for instance by undertaking to arrange their own repairs out of a common repair fund set aside out of weekly rental payments. Details of the parts of the National Consumer Council model agreement which relate to repairs and of a possible scheme under which tenants may agree to carry out their own repairs, and which might be authorised by a county court as an alternative to the statutory covenants under the Housing Act 1961, are set out in Appendix A.

2. *The Enforcement of Tenancy Agreements*

When the precise terms of the tenancy agreement between a landlord and a tenant have been established by due considera- tion of the relevant statutory provisions, of the express terms of any written or oral agreement and of any possible implied terms, the next question is how those terms may be enforced. The basic common law position was that the main remedy against a landlord or a tenant who failed to carry out the terms of the tenancy was a suit for damages and in appropriate cases for the termination of the agreement. The courts were tradi- tionally reluctant to order the parties to comply with the terms of the agreement, by issuing what is called an order for specific performance. This problem has recently been resolved by the provision under the Housing Act 1974, s. 125 that a county court may order specific performance of any repairing covenant where it considers it reasonable to do so. In addition there is the possibility of what may be termed a "self-help" remedy: where the landlord fails to carry out his obligations under the tenancy the tenant may in certain limited circum- stances do the necessary work himself and deduct the cost from the rent.

The legal rules for these methods of enforcement — court actions for specific performance, damages and termination and self-help on the part of the tenant — will be considered in turn. Since most tenants are likely to prefer a method of enforcement which results in the repairs being done, most attention will be focused on the court action for specific

performance and on self-help. For both of these an attempt
will be made to explain how action may be taken without
professional legal assistance. Further advice and guidance on
how to pursue an action in the county court without professional representation is given in an official booklet entitled
*Small Claims in the County Court: How to Sue and Defend
Actions Without a Solicitor* published by the Lord Chancel-
lor's Department and available in most citizens advice bureaux
or county court offices. Where there are additional complica-
tions on matters of rent control and security of tenure, it is
always safer to seek professional advice or assistance before
embarking on proceedings. But in many simpler cases a good
deal may be achieved by the tenant himself and lay advisers in
social work and other agencies by a few properly drafted letters
which make it clear that the writer knows the legal procedures
and is prepared to put them into operation, even if professional assistance is eventually thought necessary.

Specific performance

There were a number of reasons for the reluctance of the
courts to make orders for specific performance to require landlords to carry out their obligations to repair and maintain their
properties. It was said that the courts were not in a position to
supervise the due performance of any such order, and that a
money payment by way of compensation and the prospect of
continuing damages in the future was sufficient to induce most
landlords to take the necessary action once the matter had
been adjudicated in court. This kind of reasoning has not been
entirely swept away by the provisions of the Housing Act 1974,
s. 125. The section merely states that any existing rule of
equity restricting the scope of orders for specific performance
of a repairing covenant must be ignored, and that the court
may *in its discretion* order specific performance of a repairing
covenant, whether it relates to the premises let or to common
parts, if proceedings are initiated by a tenant. But it is now
much more likely that such orders will be granted.

Before any legal proceedings are started it is wise to ensure
that the landlord has been given due notice of the alleged
breach of covenant. There are some arguments for the view

that notice is not strictly necessary in a suit for specific performance. In practice it is highly unlikely that any court would make such an order if the landlord had not already been given a reasonable opportunity to carry out his obligations. There is no special procedure for giving notice for this purpose. The best method is to write a brief letter to the landlord or his agent, that is the person to whom the rent is paid, setting out as clearly as possible both the nature of the repair required and the term of the tenancy, whether statutory, express or implied, which requires him to do it. If there is any difficulty in ascertaining the name and address of the landlord, tenants may now rely on the provision under the Housing Act 1974, s. 121 which requires the person to whom the rent is paid to disclose the name and address of the landlord; it is a criminal offence not to comply with such a request. A sample letter, which may be adapted for most purposes, is given in Appendix B. It is always advisable to send such a letter by recorded delivery and to keep at least one copy in case the landlord or agent should deny having received it.

If a formal letter to the landlord or agent produces no results, the next step is to institute legal proceedings in the county court. Though this has traditionally been done through a solicitor, the procedure is in fact simple and straightforward and there is no reason, as already explained, why individual tenants and lay advisers should not handle it themselves. All that is required is for someone to go to the county court office, fill in the relevant forms and pay a small fee, currently of £5. If the only issue is a failure on the part of a landlord to carry out repairs, the tenant should submit "particulars of claim" alleging a breach of the terms of his tenancy and asking for the remedy of specific performance of the repairing covenants. A "request" form will then have to be filled in asking the court to serve an ordinary summons on the landlord. A specimen particulars of claim is given in Appendix C, which may again be adapted to serve most purposes. If there is any difficulty the officials in the county court office should be prepared to assist.

The service of a summons may in itself spur the landlord into action, in which case the tenant is in theory entitled to recover any costs which he has already incurred. If the landlord fails to respond or argues that he is not in breach of his

obligations, the matter will have to be heard in court. It is of
course essential for the tenant or a representative, who may be
a member of the family, a friend or a social worker, to attend
and bring all the relevant documents and letters with him. If
the action is successful and the landlord is ordered to carry out
specific repairs, the court will usually allow whatever period of
time the judge or registrar considers reasonable for the completion of the work. If the landlord still fails to comply, then it
is in theory up to the court to enforce its own order, if
necessary by punishing the landlord for contempt of court. In
practice it is unlikely that much will be done unless the tenant
informs the court office that the order has not been complied
with.

Damages

It is usual to include a claim for damages in any action for
specific performance. This is partly a result of the difficulty in
the past of obtaining decrees of specific performance, and is
not strictly necessary. Since some judges may still be reluctant
to grant orders for specific performance, however, it is probably wise to include a claim for damages.

The principle on which an award of damages is made in
cases of a failure to carry out a covenant to repair or maintain
a house or flat is that the tenant should be given a sum of
money which represents the difference in value between the
premises as they are in fact and as they should have been if the
landlord had carried out his obligations. In practice this
means that the court fixes a suitable deduction from the
weekly or monthly rent and multiples this by the number of
weeks or months since notice has been served on the landlord
that repairs are required. This rule may be illustrated by the
decision in the Liverpool tower blocks case, in which a claim
for failure to maintain a lavatory cistern was added to the
main test case on the maintenance of lifts and shutes:

Liverpool City Council v. Irwin (1976)
The tenants of a council flat claimed, as part of their
defence to a test case action by the council seeking possession of the flat on the grounds that the tenants had gone
on rent strike, that the council was in breach of its

statutory duty to maintain the lavatory in working order under the Housing Act 1961, s. 32. It was accepted that the cistern overflowed every time it was used unless the ball-cock was bent so as to reduce the supply of water to a level which rendered the flushing system ineffective. It was held in the House of Lords that this constituted a clear breach of the council's statutory duty to maintain the sanitary conveniences in proper working order; and that nominal damages of £5 in respect of the breach should be awarded.

In cases of this kind the principal issue is not usually the precise amount of the damages but the issue of responsibility and the question of who is to pay the costs of the case.

Termination

Where there is a serious breach of a tenancy agreement, a tenant instead of seeking to enforce the landlord's obligation to repair or to recover damages may terminate the tenancy. This remedy is clearly of little value in respect of continuing weekly or monthly tenancies which may be terminated at will. It may be useful in cases in which a tenant has signed a contract for a number of months or years, but wishes to or is able to move elsewhere. In such cases it is not necessary to take legal action. The tenant should simply write a formal letter to the landlord stating that in view of the landlord's failure to carry out his obligation to maintain or repair the premises after notice has been duly served on him, the tenant is hereby terminating the tenancy. If the landlord subsequently sues to recover payment for the unexpired balance of the tenancy, the tenant may then rely on the defence that he has legitimately terminated the tenancy.

Self-help

In cases where the works required to repair the premises are relatively inexpensive, the tenants may prefer to do the work themselves and charge the cost to the landlord. Tenants have the right to do this, provided the correct procedure is followed. But it is important to make it quite clear that any deduction made from the rent is specifically related to works of repair which the landlord should have carried out and that there is no question of a rent strike. Otherwise the landlord may be entitled to sue for possession of the house or flat on the ground of non-payment of rent.

The legal basis of the self-help remedy is the decision of the High Court in the case of *Lee-Parker* v. *Izzet* (1971). The facts of the case were complicated and need not be rehearsed here; but in the course of his judgement Mr. Justice Goff restated the following "ancient" common law right:

> I therefore declare that so far as the repairs are within the express or implied covenants of the landlord, the [tenants] are entitled to recoup themselves out of future rents and defend any action for payment thereof. It does not follow however that the full amount expended ... on such repairs can properly be treated as payment of rent. It is a question of fact in every case whether and to what extent the expenditure was proper. ... I must add that of course [this] right can only be exercised when and so far as the landlord is in breach and any necessary notice must have been given to him.

This doctrine has been widely relied on in law centres and has yet to be successfully challenged in the courts. The principle on which it is based has been given further judicial support in *Asco Developments Ltd.* v. *Lowes* (1978). In a preliminary judgment on the right of a tenant to defend an action to recover rent, the Vice-Chancellor, Sir Robert Megarry, held that a tenant who did and paid for work that the landlord ought to have done could set what he had paid against the landlord's claim for rent, and that the right could be exercised equally in respect of arrears of rent as in respect of future rent; the position of a tenant who had actually done repairs was much stronger in this respect than one who merely claimed a set-off in respect of an alleged failure to repair on the part of the landlord. The self-help remedy may therefore be safely relied on provided the procedural steps illustrated in the accompanying diagram and exemplified in Appendix D are carefully followed.

First it must be clearly established that the duty to repair the particular item is clearly placed on the landlord. It is preferable in this context to rely on an express or statutory term rather than on an implied term, since a court might be reluctant to endorse the doctrine in a doubtful case.

Secondly, the landlord must be given due notice of the need for repair and a reasonable time in which to do the necessary work. As in other cases it is desirable for notice to be given in writing and for copies to be kept. To make doubly sure that there is no misunderstanding on what is being done, it is desirable to serve a second notice on the landlord stating that since he has not complied with the first notice the tenant intends to carry out the work himself and to deduct the cost from future rent, in accordance with the doctrine in *Lee-Parker* v. *Izzet*. A further specimen letter for this purpose is provided in Appendix D.

Thirdly, when the time specified in the notice has expired, the tenant should proceed to have the necessary work done for him by a reputable contractor, or in appropriate cases do it himself. A written invoice and receipt should be obtained and kept; where the tenant is doing the repair himself, receipts for any materials used should be obtained and kept. It is probably better for the tenant not to claim any payment for work he does himself; though strictly speaking there is no reason why he should not, whatever charge is made may be contested by the landlord.

Finally, when the work has been completed, the tenant should use the money he would have paid in rent to pay for the cost of the repairs. The landlord should again be informed of the precise amount to be set against the rent, as in the specimen letter in Appendix D. It is better not to make any deductions or to withhold rent before the work has been done. Where substantial sums are involved and the tenant wishes to accumulate some funds in advance, the rent should be paid into a separate post office or bank account opened for the purpose and the landlord should be informed that this procedure is being followed. Alternatively a loan might be arranged for the cost of the works from a bank or credit union and any reasonable interest charge might then be added to the cost of the works.

This summary of the steps to be followed may appear unduly cautious. The principal reason for caution is the need to distinguish reliance on the self-help remedy from any form

3·1 Self-help Repairs

of rent strike. It is established law that the duty of the tenant to pay his rent is quite independent of the duty of the landlord to carry out his covenants of maintenance and repair. Tenants who withhold their rent as a sanction against a landlord who fails to do repairs accordingly risk losing whatever security of tenure they may have. The doctrine in *Lee-Parker* v. *Izzet* is strictly limited to the withholding of rent to pay for specific items of maintenance and repair.

Alternative remedies under the Public Health and Housing Acts

It must be emphasised that the remedies discussed in this chapter are not the only ones open to dissatisfied tenants. Tenants and other occupants may ask their local authorities to use their powers under the Public Health and Housing Acts to require landlords and owners to carry out specified works. Individuals may also make use of their right of direct access to the courts under the Public Health Act 1936, s. 99 to force landlords or the local authority to take some action. These alternative remedies are particularly useful for those who are not protected by the statutory covenants under the Housing Act 1961, whether because their tenancy was granted before 1961 or because they are not tenants at all but licensees. The reason for dealing separately with those remedies based on statutory, express and implied covenants in this chapter and those based on the Public Health and Housing Acts in the next is that there are important differences in the legal foundation and in the practical application of the two sets of remedies. A detailed discussion of their relative merits and of the practical choice which faces individual tenants will be found at the end of Chapter 4.

3. *Liability for Personal Injury*

The law on liability for personal injury arising from a failure to repair or maintain premises often overlaps with the law on the extent of and enforcement of repairing covenants in tenancy agreements. But there are a number of reasons for keeping the two issues distinct. In the first place the duty to compensate

for injury or damage typically arises in tort rather than in contract, and is therefore not dependent on the existence or interpretation of any contractual agreement. In the second place
the standard of responsibility imposed by the common law and
by statute is different from that imposed on landlords in
respect of their tenants. In the third place there are now strict
statutory limitations on the extent to which liability of this
kind may be excluded either by the exhibition of notices or by
contractual terms. Finally and more generally the responsibility extends to all houseowners and occupiers, including
owner-occupiers. The law on this subject is complex and
cannot be fully covered here. The point of the brief discussion
which follows is to set out in simple terms the extent of the
liability which may arise, and thus to clarify the type of risk
against which the various categories of owner and occupier
should insure themselves.

Occupiers' liability in tort

The legal basis of the liability of owners and occupiers to
compensate anyone injured on their premises is the common
duty of care currently prescribed under the Occupiers'
Liability Act 1957. This duty is said to arise in tort rather than
in contract, in that it is not dependent upon any prior agreement between the owner or occupier and the person injured.
The duty is owed to everyone who comes onto the premises,
even on occasions to trespassers, except in so far as it is validly
excluded or waived. Where there is a breach of this duty, any
person who suffers injury or death, or whose goods are
damaged, may sue for damages as a result. Such a person is
said to have a right of action in tort or negligence for the
wrong done to him by the person responsible.

The person primarily responsible, as the title of the statute
indicates, is the occupier. This may be an owner-occupier or in
the case of rented property a lessee, tenant or licensee. But
where the landlord of rented premises is under an obligation to
maintain or repair the premises, whether by an express or
implied term in the tenancy agreement or by any statutory
provision, liability in tort for any breach of that duty is owed
by the landlord to any person lawfully on the premises

(Defective Premises Act 1972, s. 4). When the landlord expressly or by implication reserves a right of entry, such responsibility is readily inferred (see *Mint* v. *Good* (above)). This means that liability is often split between the occupier and the landlord: the landlord is responsible for injury or damage arising from any breach of his duty to maintain or repair, and the occupier is responsible for any other breach of the common duty of care. For example the landlord might be responsible for any injury to a tenant or a member of the tenant's family or a visitor who slipped on a loose doorstep, since that would be included under the statutory covenant under the Housing Act 1961, s. 32, while the tenant might be responsible if the same person slipped on a similarly defective step in the tenant's garden. In addition under the Defective Premises Act 1972 a person who builds or converts any dwelling is responsible for any injury which results from any failure on his part to carry out his work in a workmanlike or professional manner and with proper materials. In such case any liability shifts from the occupier or landlord to the building contractor or architect.

The standard of care

The standard of care prescribed under the Occupiers' Liability Act 1957 is that of the reasonable man.

The common duty of care is a duty to take such care as in all the circumstances of the case is reasonable to see that the visitor will be reasonably safe in using the premises for the purposes for which he is invited or permitted to be there. (s.2(2)).

In general terms this means that the person seeking to recover damages must show that someone has been negligent. If no negligence or fault of any kind can be proved to the satisfaction of a court, then the injured person must bear his own loss. More specific rules are then laid down, both under the Act and by decisions of the courts, in respect of particular classes of people, notably children, to whom a higher standard of care is owed, and trespassers, to whom a minimal duty of care to avoid especially obvious dangers is owed.

In so far as the maintenance and repair of premises is

concerned, the duty of common care will frequently be identical to that owed under the provisions of a lease or tenancy agreement. Most of the court cases on the interpretation of landlords' statutory, express or implied covenants have in fact arisen in the context of personal injury claims, as will be clear from the examples given above. The same limitations on the extent of that liability as have already been discussed have been held to apply. This means that no liability will generally be imposed on the landlord unless he knows or should have known of the existence of a defect for which he is responsible. Where a tenant fails to give due notice to the landlord of an obvious defect, the tenant himself might even be held liable for failing to exercise common care by informing the landlord of the need for repair. In the case of latent defects, such as the ceiling in the case of *O'Brien* v. *Robinson* (see above), it may be held that no-one is liable since no-one has been at fault. This extension of the notice rule to personal injury claims has been criticised on the ground that the intention of Parliament in passing the relevant sections of the Housing Acts was to place full responsibility on landlords for certain aspects of the maintenance and repair of their premises. But the fault principle is deeply embedded in the law. An absolute duty of care is imposed on owners and occupiers only in certain cases in which inherently dangerous activities are being carried on on the premises.

The exclusion of liability

Until 1977 it was permissible for occupiers and landlords to limit their responsibility for personal injury and damage by the insertion of exclusion clauses in tenancy agreements or else by putting up notices on their premises. Liability for breach of the statutory covenants under the Housing Acts could probably not be avoided in this way, since as has been seen these covenants are imposed regardless of the terms of any tenancy agreement and the Occupiers' Liability Act 1957 extended the protection given to the tenant to members of the tenant's family and to all lawful visitors. But all other forms of liability could be avoided or limited by properly drafted clauses or notices.

Substantial changes in the law in this respect have been made under the Unfair Contract Terms Act 1977: exclusion of any kind, whether by the terms of a contract or by putting up a notice, is now prohibited in respect of any claim for personal injury based upon negligence, which is expressly stated to include any breach of the common duty of care in respect of occupiers' liability (s. 2). And in respect of claims for other loss or damage resulting from a similar breach of duty liability may only be excluded or restricted if the term or notice satisfies the test of reasonableness. This means in practice that neither landlords nor owner-occupiers nor tenants can avoid liability for an injury resulting from a culpable failure to carry out their repairing obligations, and conversely that whenever someone is injured as a result of such a culpable failure, some- one must be liable. This may be either the person who is responsible for the particular aspect of maintenance or repair, or if that person has no reason to know of and has not been informed of the need for repair any other person who has a duty to the person injured. The position in respect of damage to property is even less clear in that there is little indication in the Unfair Contract Terms Act of the types of limitation or restriction of liability which might meet the test of reasonable- ness. It is likely that the courts will permit owners, landlords and tenants to limit their liability in this respect to stated sums, as for instance in the case of notices restricting liability in respect of items left in cloakrooms to a maximum of £20 per item.

Liability and insurance

It will be clear from this brief account that the principle of fault liability creates a good deal of uncertainty and legal com- plexity in this sphere as in others. It is rarely possible to give a precise answer in advance as to who if anyone will be liable to compensate persons who suffer personal injury or loss as a result of defective maintenance or repair. Owner-occupiers, landlords and tenants alike may be held liable depending on the circumstances of the case. In practice actions are rarely started against low-income tenants, if only because they would be unable to meet any substantial award against them. But owner-occupiers and landlords and some better off tenants may find themselves being sued in circumstances which they did not in any way foresee, for instance if a tradesman or visitor suffers injury while on their premises even from a relative minor defect which the occupiers have learned to live with. The amount of money which may be involved may be very substantial. Awards of up to £50,000 are now quite common in cases where serious brain damage is caused by falls, and awards of several thousands of pounds may be made for broken limbs.

The proper course of action for all owners and occupiers to take is to insure themselves against liability of this kind. Most simple household policies of the type taken out by owner-occupiers and some tenants include cover against occupiers' liability, which is sometimes also referred to as public liability. The cost of this cover is minimal in comparison with the premiums for cover against fire and other risks to the insured person's own property. It is not particularly satisfactory to have to recommend that all tenants and licensees, as well as land-lords and owner-occupiers, should take out occupiers' liability insurance. But given the high incidence of accidents in the home and the current state of the law, no other advice is possible. The Pearson Commission on Civil Liability and Compensation for Personal Injury estimated that there were about 100,000 accidents each year attributable to defective premises compared with about 300,000 attributable to motor vehicles, for which insurance is compulsory; the Commission concluded, somewhat surprisingly in view of these figures, that occupiers' liability did not constitute a social problem serious enough to require special action; accordingly it did not recommend any change in the law to impose strict or no fault liability or to make insurance compulsory (Cmnd. 7054 (1978), paras. 1565-67).

Further Reading

For a general account of the law of landlord and tenant with a practical rather than a legalistic approach see Martin Partington, *Landlord and Tenant* (1975), Ch. 1.

For a more specific discussion of the enforcement of statutory covenants see Hilary Fassnidge and Paul Robson, "Housing Repairs in Context", *LAG Bulletin* July 1977, pp. 156-159. For a more detailed historical discussion of the development of the statutory covenant see J.I. Reynolds, "Statutory Covenants of Fitness and Repair: Social Legislation and the Judges," (1974) 37 *M.L.R.* 377, and the rejoinder by M.J. Robinson, (1976) 39 *M.L.R.* 43.

4 Compulsory Repair and Improvement under the Public Health and Housing Acts

The remedies discussed in this chapter are essentially different from those dealt with in Chapter 3. They are not directly dependent on the existence of a landlord-tenant relationship and the repairing covenants which that relationship usually creates but on the enforcement of reasonable standards of maintenance and repair in the public interest. Under the Public Health Acts, as has been explained in Chapter 2, local authorities may require any person to abate a statutory nuisance which constitutes a threat to any person's health or safety. This has been regularly applied to most forms of disrepair in dwelling houses. Under the Housing Acts local authorities have further powers to deal with houses which are unfit for human habitation, houses which lack basic amenities, and since 1969 houses which are not unfit but in substantial disrepair.

These powers are discretionary in the sense that the initiation of the relevant procedures is regarded as primarily a matter for the local authority. But there are means by which individuals may set the wheels in motion. Under the Public Health Acts the procedure designed by Sir John Simon to permit local activists to bring before their local magistrates matters which constituted a threat to public health but which were not being effectively dealt with by the local authority may now be relied on by individual tenants and licensees as a means of forcing landlords and local authority housing departments to carry out repairs. The fact that under the Housing Acts there is a statutory duty on local authorities to prevent people from living in unfit houses may also be relied on, though less simply and directly, to put pressure on local authorities to use their powers.

In this chapter the basic legal rules and procedures on the

abatement of statutory nuisances under the Public Health Acts, on compulsory repair notices under the Housing Act 1957, and on compulsory improvement notices under the Housing Act 1974 will be set out in turn. The object is not to give a comprehensive legal analysis of the duties of local authorities under the Public Health and Housing Acts. Some other related aspects of the Housing Acts, notably in respect of houses in multiple occupation and area rehabilitation programmes, will be dealt with in subsequent chapters. But no attempt will be made to cover the whole range of public health powers and duties, nor the administration and financing of council housing. The specific focus on the various forms of compulsory repair and improvement notices, and the concluding analysis on their interrelationship and practical utility is intended primarily as a guide to individual tenants and landlords and their advisers, but may also perhaps be of use to local authority officials. As in Chapter 3, specimen letters and documents are provided in appendices.

1. *The Statutory Nuisance Procedure*

The basis of the procedure for dealing with housing disrepair under the Public Health Acts is the concept of a statutory nuisance. When the existence of a statutory nuisance is established there is an obligation on local authorities to see that it is abated, and private individuals have an independent right to bring the matter before a magistrates court.

What is a statutory nuisance?

The most directly relevant part of the current definition of a statutory nuisance under the Public Health Act 1936, s. 92 is that which covers "any premises in such a state as to be prejudicial to health or a nuisance." But the definition also extends to such matters as accumulations and deposits, and animals kept in such a way as to be prejudicial to health or a nuisance, and under the Noise Abatement Act 1960 to noise and vibration. Until recently this formulation was somewhat loosely interpreted to cover virtually any kind of disrepair in an occupied dwelling. It was held in one case that anything which could cause discomfort to occupants might constitute a statutory nuisance (*Betts* v. *Penge Urban District Council* (1942)). A number of recent test cases promoted by tenants associations and law centres, however, have resulted in a more precise and on occasions legalistic approach by the higher courts. In particular it is now necessary to distinguish between conditions which may be prejudicial to health and those which may constitute a nuisance:

National Coal Board v. *Thorne* (*1976*)

An environmental health officer of the Neath District Council served an abatement notice on the National Coal Board in respect of a house in which the windows, rain gutters and skirting boards were found to be faulty or rotten. The notice alleged that these conditions constituted a nuisance; there was no suggestion that they might prejudice the health of the occupants. It was held on appeal from the local magistrates, who had ordered the abatement of the nuisance, that the two limbs of the definition must be kept distinct, following the decision in *Salford City Council* v. *McNally* (1975) (see below); that the defects alleged could not constitute a nuisance, since they affected only the occupants of the house; and that consequently, since no prejudice to the occupants' health had been alleged, the abatement order must be quashed.

The practical effect of cases like this may easily be exaggerated. In many areas there has been no observable change in the approach of local authorities and magistrates. But it is safer to deal separately with the two limbs of the definition.

The broader and generally more useful limb is that based on prejudice to health. The prejudice may be to any person provided that it arises from the physical condition of the premises. In the context of simple disrepair it is clearly the health of the occupants which is most likely to be relevant, though there may also be some risk to passers-by from falling slates and masonry. Prejudice to health is generally given a liberal interpretation, though there is as yet no authority for the view that it should extend to "a state of complete physical, mental and social well-being and not merely the absence of diseases or infirmity" in accordance with the Constitution of the World Health Organisation. Medical evidence, however, is not usually required. The most obvious risks to health from disrepair are those caused by defective sanitation and drains and any interference with the supply of drinking water. Any form of structural instability which might result in the collapse of walls, floors, stairs or ceilings or the falling of plaster, fixtures and fittings is also clearly covered in that occupants or passers-by might be injured as a result. Rotten woodwork, particularly in floors and stairs, falls into the same category. Another major category is dampness which may likewise affect the health of occupants, especially if there are children or elderly persons. This covers leaking roofs, defective guttering and pointing, rotten or ill-fitting windows and doors, and the absence of proper protection from rising damp. The conditions disclosed in the case of *National Coal Board* v. *Thorne* (above) might well have fallen into this category if the point had been argued. Dampness resulting from condensation may also be covered if it can be said to arise from some defect in the construction or insulation of the premises. A number of abatement orders have been issued against local authorities in cases of this kind (*Tusting* v. *London Borough of Kensington* (1976)). Where condensation results merely from the production of excessive water vapour within the dwelling, on the other hand, for instance by drying clothes, it may be more difficult to show that it results from the state of the premises rather than the activities of the occupants. In such cases the outcome is likely to depend partly on the attitude of local environmental health officers and magistrates, partly on whether it can be shown that there is some deficiency of design or construction in the building, and partly on the availability of practicable measures to lessen the problem. It is clearly settled, however, that defective decoration will not normally be covered:

Springett v. *Harold* (1954)
An abatement notice was served in respect of a house in which the paint in the first floor rooms and landings was stained and peeling off. The magistrates held that since the premises were not damp or verminous or otherwise unfit for human habitation or injurious to health, the notice could not be enforced. This decision was upheld on appeal.

The second limb of the definition, based on the common

law concept of nuisance, is less directly applicable to disrepair.
A nuisance at common law is an interference with the rights of
adjoining property owners (a private nuisance) or with the
safety and comfort of the public at large (a public nuisance).
Accordingly loose slates or gutters which might fall onto
adjoining property or onto the street may constitute both a
private and a public nuisance. So too may a constant stream of
water from leaking pipes or gutters. So too may accumulations
or activities which cause offensive smell or noise. It is not
entirely clear how far all such nuisances may be dealt with by
the summary procedures under the Public Health Acts as
opposed to an ordinary common law action. It has been
suggested in some cases that abatement notices and orders
under the Public Health Acts may be issued only in respect of
nuisances which cause some prejudice to health:

Coventry Council v. Cartwright (1975)
A local resident complained about piles of household
refuse and building waste on a local authority building
site. The local authority removed the household refuse
from time to time, but refused to deal with the building
waste. The local magistrates issued an abatement order
on the ground that the accumulation of building waste
was not only prejudicial to health in that people who
entered the site might injure themselves on it, but also
a nuisance in that it was unsightly to local residents. On
appeal by the local authority the order was quashed:
"an accumulation or deposit" under s. 92 of the Public
Health Act 1936 was prejudicial to health only if it was
likely to cause a risk of disease or if it might attract
vermin, but not merely from the risk of injury to people
walking on it or children playing on it; nor could the
visual impact of the waste constitute a nuisance.

On the other hand abatement notices and orders have regularly
been issued under the Public Health Acts in respect of noisy
trade activities and animals without any specific health risk being established, and noise and vibration have been expressly
stated to be statutory nuisances under the Noise Abatement Act
1960. The outcome in cases which fall outside the established
categories of disrepair and health risk will depend largely on the
policy of local environmental health officials and magistrates.

It should also be noted that certain other forms of disrepair and dilapidation may be dealt with as if they were statutory nuisances, though they are not strictly defined as such. Under the Public Health Act 1936, s. 39 abatement notices and orders may be served and enforced in respect of any form of unsatisfactory drainage, including insufficient cesspools, private sewers, drains, soil pipes, rain water pipes, spouts, sinks and other necessary appliances provided for the building. This is very widely used as an alternative to section 92. In addition under the Public Health Act 1936, s. 58 owners may be required to carry out works to make safe any dangerous building or structure, and under the Public Health Act 1961, s. 27 owners may be required to repair or restore, or if they prefer to demolish and clear, any building or structure which is "by reason of its ruinous or dilapidated condition seriously detrimental to the amenities of the neighbourhood." These provisions may be used to deal with such things as bulging garden walls and dilapidated huts and garages more directly than by alleging that they constitute a statutory nuisance.

Enforcement by local authorities

Local authorities have a statutory duty to inspect their areas for statutory nuisances under the Public Health Act 1936 (s. 91). This is one of the principle functions of Environmental Health Departments. In some areas, particularly those designated for clearance or rehabilitation, house to house inspections are carried out. But local authorities are generally dependent on complaints from members of the public or tenants. Once the local authority is satisfied that a statutory nuisance exists it must serve an abatement notice on the person responsible (s. 93). This notice must specify the nature of the nuisance and give the person on whom it is served a reasonable time to deal with it; it may also specify the works which the local authority considers necessary. It should be noted that some local authorities also serve what are called "informal notices" or "intimations." There is no legal basis for this practice. An informal notice is merely a warning that the statutory powers may be used if the matter is not dealt with.

The person on whom the abatement notice should be served

is "the person by whose act, default or sufferance the nuisance
arises or continues" (s. 93). In the case of defective maintenance or disrepair it may be taken that this person is the
owner-occupier or in the case of rented premises the person on
whom the duty to repair is cast by the tenancy agreement. In
respect of structural defects, however, it is expressly provided
that the notice shall be served on the owner (s. 93(a)). Where
the person responsible cannot be found the notice may be
served on either the owner or the occupier, unless it is clear
that neither is responsible (s. 93(b)). Accordingly where the
precise position on repairs is not clear, the local authority may
serve the notice on either the landlord or the tenant or licensee and leave it to the recipient to object if he is not the person
responsible. In practice most Environmental Health Departments prefer to serve notices in respect of rented premises on
the landlord or his agent, and often refrain from serving
notices based on simple disrepair on owner-occupiers unless
there is some immediate danger to the public or to other
occupants. Where it is clear that neither the owner nor the
occupier is responsible and the person who is responsible
cannot be found there is a residual duty on the local authority
itself to take steps to abate the nuisance (s. 93(b)). If it fails to
do so, it may eventually be required to act by court order, as
explained below.

The service of an abatement notice often has the desired
effect of inducing the landlord to carry out the necessary
repairs. If it does not, the local authority must bring the
matter before the local magistrates court (s. 94(1)). This is done
by means of a formal complaint to the court, which then serves
a summons on the person named in the complaint to appear
on a stated day for the hearing of the case. The proceedings at
the hearing are likely to be relatively straightforward. The
environmental health officer will outline the background to
the case, explain the nature of the alleged nuisance and ask the
magistrates to make an appropriate order. The landlord or his
representative will then be given an opportunity to reply. He
may, for instance, argue that there is no nuisance, or that the
tenant or some other person is responsible for it, or that more
time is needed to carry out the necessary work. There will not
normally be any need for the tenant or other complainant to

attend the hearing, though in certain cases he may be called as a witness by the local authority or the landlord.

If the court decides that there is a statutory nuisance and that the person on whom the notice was served is responsible, it must make a formal order for its abatement within a specified period of days or weeks (s. 94(2)); it may also require the person responsible to pay the costs of the hearing, and may impose a fine of up to £200 (s. 94(2)-(3)). If the abatement order is not complied with the court may impose a further fine of up to £400 plus up to £50 per day until it is complied with (s. 95). Where neither the person responsible nor the owner or occupier can be found, the court may order the local authority itself to abate the nuisance (s. 94(6)). Alternatively the local authority may itself decide to carry out the works in default (s. 95(2)) and recover the cost from the person responsible (s. 96). The court has a further power to prohibit the continued habitation of any building until it has been made fit for habitation (s. 94(2)), but this is not often used. The only major loophole in the general statutory policy that once a statutory nuisance is proved it must be abated by one or other of these means is the discretion of the court to postpone the operation of any abatement order if no useful public purpose would be served by immediate enforcement:

> *Nottingham District Council v. Newton (1974)*
> The tenant of a house in a slum clearance area wrote to the local authority asking them to serve an abatement notice on her landlord, a local housing association, in respect of various items of disrepair. The local authority served a notice in respect of a few minor items which were duly carried out. The tenant then made a complaint direct to the magistrates asking for an abatement order in respect of matters not covered in the local authority notice. The magistrates upheld the complaint and ordered the local authority to carry out the additional works within three months. On appeal by the local authority, it was held that while the magistrates were required to make an abatement order, they had a discretion on the timing of any works; since they had a duty "to look at the whole circumstances of the case and to try and make an order which was ... sensible and just having

regard to the entire prevailing situation," they had been wrong to ignore the pending clearance scheme; the case was remitted to the magistrates to make a new order, with a suggestion that the abatement order might be postponed until the clearance order was confirmed.

These powers are widely used and are generally reasonably effective. Large urban authorities regularly serve hundreds or thousands of abatement notices each year, and most are prepared to use their default powers to ensure compliance. The main problem is cumulative delay, both in bringing owners who do not comply with notices before the magistrates and in the use of default powers. In some areas there is a waiting period of several months for cases of this kind. Yet under the standard procedure which has just been set out the local authority cannot carry out the prescribed works in default in cases where the landlord is clearly the person responsible until an abatement order has been made by the magistrates, and has not been complied with. To permit more effective enforcement many local authorities obtained special powers under local statutes to enable them to carry out prescribed works in default much more quickly where landlords or owners failed to comply with abatement notices.

A general power to this effect has now been granted to all local authorities under the Public Health Act 1961, s. 26. This authorises local authorities to serve what is termed a "nine-day" notice in cases where unreasonable delay in remedying a statutory nuisance would result from using the standard procedure under the Public Health Act 1936. If this notice is not complied with in nine days the local authority may then carry out the works in default without taking the case before the magistrates, and collect the cost from the person responsible. But if the person on whom the notice is served serves a counter-notice within seven days, stating that he intends to remedy the specified defects, the local authority may only carry out the works in default if he fails to start or complete the works within a reasonable period. Any dispute on whether the local authority has acted reasonably in using this expedited procedure must then be resolved in the magistrates court when the local authority seeks to recover the cost of the works. If the magistrates consider that the procedure has been abused, they may refuse to order the landlord to make any payment. The advantages of greater speed in enforcement are thus offset by the risk that the full cost of the works may fall on the local authority. The use of the procedure under the Public Health Act 1961 in preference to those under the Public Health Act 1936 varies widely from area to area, depending on the attitude of senior environmental health officers and of local magistrates. But tenants of landlords who have in the past been dilatory in carrying out repairs in response to court orders or abatement notices should make a point of asking their Environmental Health Department to use it.

Individual enforcement

These procedures for official enforcement, illustrated in the accompanying diagram, provide a relatively speedy, straightforward and effective remedy for tenants in areas where the Environmental Health Department is prepared to use its powers to full effect. The fact that all the necessary legal and administrative work is carried out by the local authority is an additional advantage, particularly for those who are reluctant to become involved in legal proceedings on their own account or who are not eligible for legal aid (see Andrew Arden, *Housing: Security and Rent Control*, app. 2). All that is required from the tenant is a visit or telephone call to the Environmental Health Department of his local authority.

Where the Environmental Health Department is dilatory or unhelpful the position is much less satisfactory. This is most likely to be a problem for council tenants. Most Environmental Health Departments take the view that it is legally impossible for one department of a local authority to take proceedings against another, so that formal abatement notices cannot be served on their own Housing Departments. When a complaint from a council tenant is received and it appears that the defects are such as to constitute a statutory nuisance, the practice in most areas is for the Environmental Health Department to send an informal notice or memorandum to the Housing Department. Since in many cases the tenant will have already complained a number of times to the Housing Department, this is unlikely to have much immediate impact.

4·1 Public Health Act

PRIVATE SECTOR

PUBLIC SECTOR

STATUTORY NUISANCE
Private landlord | Council Housing

Tenant complains to E.H.Dept.

Tenant complains to Envir. Health Dept.

Informal memo to Housing Dept.

Direct complaint to Court by Tenant
S.99

URGENT NOTICE to Owner to do work in 9 days
S.26

ABATEMENT NOTICE served by E. Health Dept. on private landlord
S.93

Council does work

MAGISTRATES COURT
S.94 | S.99

Court order to comply plus FINE and / or COSTS
S.94

Owner complies

L.A. does work in default and collects cost from Owner

Owner complies after court order

In such cases the tenant may have to fall back on his right under the Public Health Act 1936, s. 99 to bring a case before the magistrates court on his own initiative. The procedure for this purpose is similar to that for complaints by the local authority except that no abatement notice need be served. It is nonetheless wise to make a formal request to the local authority to take steps to have the nuisance abated before embarking on an individual action. A specimen letter for this purpose is included in Appendix E. If this does not have the desired effect, the next step is to bring the matter before the local magistrates court by way of what in procedural terms is called an "information". This is technically a criminal rather than a civil proceeding under the terms of the Magistrates Court Act 1952, s. 44, but it has been held in the High Court that since a person who brings proceedings of this kind may ask the court to impose any of the orders, including a fine, which the local authority might ask for, a criminal information is more appropriate than a civil complaint (*R.* v. *Newham Justices, ex p. Hunt* (1976). In practical terms this means that the tenant or his advisers must send to the court office two documents, a formal information and a statement giving full details of the nature of the statutory nuisance alleged and of the remedy requested (see Appendix E). If the defendant is not the local authority as landlord, a copy of these documents should also be sent to the local authority with a request to attend at the hearing in case the magistrates may wish to hear their views.

The procedure at the hearing will not be essentially different from that described above, except that the tenant or his representative must outline the background to the case and call any necessary witnesses. If the magistrates find that the defects which are proved constitute a statutory nuisance, they may order the landlord, which in the case of council housing will be the local authority, to abate it and impose a fine or costs as appropriate. The magistrates are also specifically authorised under section 99 to order the local authority to abate a nuisance for which some other person is responsible, leaving it to the local authority to recover the cost from that person. This power, which may only be exercised after hearing the views of the local authority, is somewhat wider than that under section 94(6) (see above) which permits the court to order the local authority to carry out the works only where the person responsible cannot be found. The reason for this difference is presumably that the local authority may be regarded as having failed to carry out its duty to secure the abatement of the nuisance on its own initiative.

This right of individual action under section 99, which is also illustrated in the diagram, has been widely used in recent years in respect of defective council housing. One reason for this was the fact that it was a good deal easier to obtain what amounts to a decree of specific performance under the statutory nuisance procedure than by suing for the enforcement of the statutory covenants under the Housing Acts. This is a less obvious advantage following the provisions of the Housing Act 1974, s. 125 removing the equitable bars on specific performance (see Chapter 3). The procedure for laying an information in a magistrates court under section 99 is not inherently any simpler than that for taking an action to enforce a repairing covenant in a county court. It may nonetheless be the only effective remedy for those council tenants who are not protected by the statutory covenants under the Housing Act 1961 since their tenancies were granted before 1961 or by those under the Housing Act 1957 since their rent exceeds the statutory figures. It may also be the only effective remedy for those tenants of private landlords who are likewise prevented from relying on the statutory covenants and whose local Environmental Health Department is dilatory and reluctant to carry out works in default when landlords fail to comply with abatement notices or orders.

2. *Unfitness and Compulsory Repair Notices under the Housing Act 1957*

Local authorities have an entirely separate set of powers under the Housing Act 1957 to require owner-occupiers and landlords to carry out prescribed repairs. These powers, which date back to the housing legislation of 1885, were originally founded on the concept of unfitness and were closely tied to the procedures for dealing with groups or areas of unfit housing. But they may also be used in respect of individual unfit houses, and since 1969 in respect of houses which are not unfit but are in substantial disrepair. The principal advantage in using these powers compared with those under the Public Health Acts is that more comprehensive works may be prescribed with a view to bringing the whole house up to a reasonable standard of fitness or repair. On the other hand there is no simple procedure comparable to those for the abatement of statutory nuisances and the enforcement of tenancy agreements by which individual tenants may require their local authority to have the house repaired. The mandatory nature of the duty imposed on local authorities to deal with unfit houses means that individuals and action groups can usually force a local authority to take some action if a house is clearly unfit. But the end result, as will be seen, may often be closure and rehousing rather than the completion of the repairs which the complainant originally envisaged. This is a complex area of law in which it is difficult to foresee the eventual outcome of any proceedings. The account which follows is an attempt to explain the essentials of the various procedures without concealing the practical difficulties which they may give rise to.

Unfitness

The underlying intention of the Housing Acts is that no-one should be allowed to live in a house which is unfit for human habitation. This is directly reflected in the current definition of unfitness under the Housing Act 1957, s. 4: a dwelling is statutorily unfit where it is "so far defective" in one or more of a list of nine items as to be "not reasonably suitable for occupation." The nine items are: (i) repair; (ii) stability; (iii) freedom from damp; (iv) internal arrangement; (v) natural lighting; (vi) ventilation; (vii) water supply; (viii) drainage and sanitary conveniences; and (ix) facilities for preparation and cooking of food and disposal of waste water. It is further specifically provided that all "back-to-back" houses shall be deemed to be unfit (s. 5).

It is clear from even the briefest consideration of this definition that the designation of a house as unfit is a highly subjective matter. The report of the Denington Committee, *Our*

Older Homes: a call for action (1966), expressed concern over the variation in standards from area to area and recommended the introduction of a more explicit set of guidelines. These were relayed to local authorities in Circular 69/67. It was suggested, for instance, that to render a house unfit any disrepair must be a threat to the health of the occupants or cause them serious inconvenience, if only from a multiplicity of small items. Similarly imprecise guidelines were suggested for each of the other eight items. Nor have the courts been able to give much assistance in the various cases which have come before them, notably on the interpretation of what is now the statutory covenant under the Housing Act 1957, s. 6 requiring landlords of houses let at low rents to keep them fit for human habitation (see Chapter 3). The judges have not been able to do more than give a suitable paraphrase of the statutory definition and then make an ad hoc decision on the facts, as in the following example in which a house with a broken sash-cord was held to be unfit:

> ### *Summers v. Salford Corporation (1943)*
> The tenant of a council flat was injured when trying to close a bedroom window which had been jammed open because the sash-cord had broken. The tenant, who had given notice of the defect, sued for damages. It was held in the House of Lords that in the particular circumstances the failure of the council to repair the window was sufficient to render the house unfit since the bedroom was one of only two and was not reasonably suitable for occupation with the window jammed open or shut; Lord Atkin added by way of example that "a burst or a leaking pipe, a displaced slate or tile, a stopped drain, a rotten stair tread might each of them until repair make a house unfit to live in, though each might be quickly and cheaply repaired; but disrepair to a single room would not be sufficient unless the effect was to render the whole house not reasonably fit for human habitation, as in the case before the court."

The approach of the courts, however, has typically been more strict in cases involving claims for damages for breach of the statutory covenant of fitness than in cases where the issue has been the enforcement of compulsory repair, closure or demolition and the compensation of owners as a result. The eventual decision of environmental health officers, who make the initial designation, and of judges on appeal is likely to depend as much on the particular context in which the designation is being made as on the precise physical condition of the house.

Requiring an inspection

The designation of unfit houses is not wholly a matter for local authorities. There is a procedure by which individuals may initiate the inspection of a house to see whether it is unfit. Under the Housing Act 1957 a justice of the peace with jurisdiction in the area may make a written complaint to a local authority in respect of a particular house or area of houses, requiring the local authority to carry out an inspection and make a report on whether it is unfit (s. 157(2)). To set this procedure in motion it should be sufficient for an individual or action group to give sufficient evidence to a justice of the peace to indicate that a particular house or area of houses is unfit. In practical terms this will involve carrying out a detailed survey of the premises and compiling a written report on its condition, which may then be given to the justice of the peace. Models for this purpose are set out in Appendix F.

This procedure has been used with a good deal of success in recent years as a means of forcing local authorities to act in cases of really bad housing. In many areas it is the best and quickest method of securing a closing order and rehousing for occupants. But a closing order and the attendant duty to rehouse is only one of the possible consequences of a decision by the local authority that a house is unfit. The local authority must also consider whether the house can be made fit at reasonable expense, and if it can, must serve a compulsory repair notice on the owner. And if it cannot be made fit at reasonable expense the local authority instead of making a closing order and rehousing the occupants may decide to compulsorily purchase the house and retain it in use for the time being. Before embarking on the procedure under section 157 or otherwise drawing attention to the unfitness of a house it is important to have a clear understanding of the possible consequences.

Compulsory repair notices for unfit houses (s. 9(1))

When a house which is not in a designated clearance area is found to be unfit by a local authority and it appears that it may be made fit at reasonable expense, the local authority must serve a compulsory repair notice under the Housing Act 1957, s. 9(1). The notice must set out in detail the works which are required to make the house fit and state a reasonable time of not less than 21 days within which the works are to be completed. Reasonable expense for this purpose, as explained in greater detail in Appendix J, means any amount which is less than the net increase in the market value of the house as a result of the completion of the prescribed works; the relevant cost of the repairs, however, is the net cost to the owner after the receipt of any grant which may be payable. The notice must be served on the person who has control of the house. This clearly covers owner-occupiers and is expressly stated to cover any person who receives the rent from the house either on his own account or as agent or trustee for someone else (s. 39). That person is responsible for carrying out the prescribed works regardless of the terms of any tenancy agreement, though he may presumably recover the cost of such works from any other person who has a legal obligation to do them.

If the person in control of the house objects to the repair notice he may appeal within 21 days to the county court on any relevant ground, for instance that the house is not unfit, that the works prescribed are excessive or that they cannot be carried out at reasonable expense (s. 11). The judge then has a wide discretion to confirm, vary or quash the notice. If there is no appeal, or if on appeal the notice is confirmed, the works must then be carried out by the person in control of the house within the prescribed period. If they are not the local authority may carry them out in default and charge the cost of doing so to the person in control (s. 10). If there is no further appeal, the amount claimed may be recovered either as a simple civil debt, which may be secured on the property, or by means of a regular deduction from the rent payable by the occupier (s. 10(5)). If on appeal the court decides that the prescribed works cannot be carried out at reasonable expense, the local authority may then be authorised to compulsorily purchase the house (s. 12) (see below).

This intricate procedure is illustrated in the accompanying diagram. Its administration is usually entrusted to the Environmental Health Department, but in some areas it may be the responsibility of the section of the Housing Department which deals with slum clearance. Like other procedures under the Housing Acts, the frequency with which it is used and its effectiveness is largely dependent on the policy of the local authority and the attitude of senior officials. The procedure can be used to good effect provided the local authority is prepared to use its power to carry out the works in default, which is the only effective sanction against those who fail to comply. There is a marked reluctance in many authorities, however, to enforce notices in this way as a matter of course and the proportion of notices which are pursued to completion of the works is often extremely small. The rising cost of building work in recent years has also made it difficult in many cases to prescribe works which will render the house fully fit but which will not also exceed the reasonable expense criterion. And if a notice is served which in the event turns out not to be capable of being complied with at reasonable expense, there is a strong likelihood, as will be seen, that the local authority will have to close the house, and rehouse and compensate the occupants. In some cases this may give the landlord a chance to get rid of his sitting tenants and sell the house for rehabilitation by owner-occupiers at a substantial profit. The net result is that relatively few notices are currently served under s. 9(1).

Closing orders and compulsory purchase of unfit houses

In cases where the local authority takes the view that an unfit house, whether owner-occupied or rented, cannot be made fit at reasonable expense, then an entirely different set of procedures, also included in the diagram, should be followed. The local authority must call all persons with a legal interest in the house, including the tenant, to what is called a "time and place" meeting at which the future of the house will be discussed with representatives of the local authority (s. 16). If the owner of the house wishes to spend the money necessary to make it fit, he may give an undertaking to the local authority

4·2 Unfit Procedure

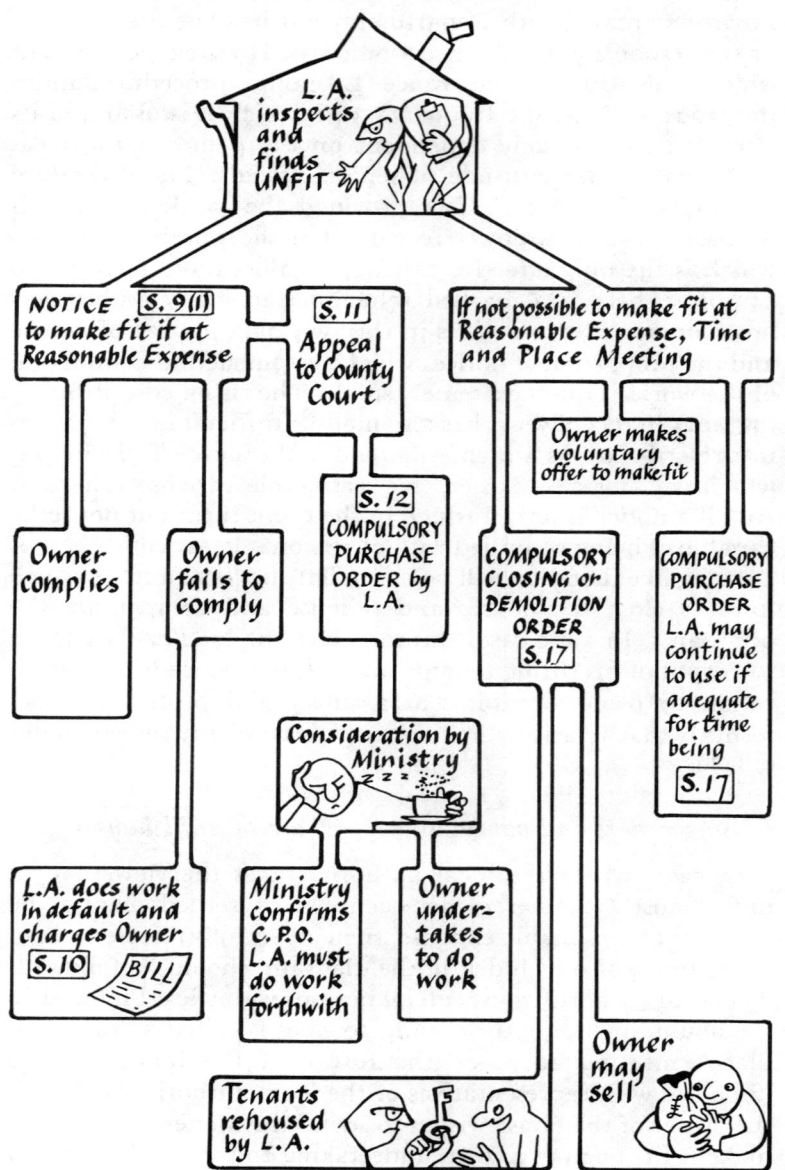

either to carry out the necessary works within a specified period or else not to use the house for occupation until such works have been done (s. 16(4)). If such an undertaking is not given, or not accepted by the local authority, which has absolute discretion in such matters, the local authority must *either* make a closing order or a demolition order (s. 17(1)), in which case the occupants must be rehoused and compensated by the local authority under the Land Compensation Act 1973 (see Chapter 8), *or else* purchase the house voluntarily or compulsorily if it is capable of being made suitable for temporary occupation (ss. 17(2) and 29).

The use of these powers, like those of compulsory repair to unfit houses, depends largely on the policy of the local authority. It will be clear from the figures given in Chapter 1 (see Table 1.1) that no local authority makes a serious attempt to apply the letter of the law in this context, despite the fact that it has been held that they have a statutory duty to pursue the relevant procedures in respect of all houses (*R.* v. *Kerrier District Council, ex p. Guppys (Bridport) Ltd.* (1976) (see below). In some areas closing orders are quite frequently used or threatened as a means of inducing landlords to improve conditions in their houses or parts of their houses, particularly basement flats. In such areas voluntary undertakings to make the premises fit will be readily accepted and the powers of compulsory purchase are unlikely to be used. They are rarely used against owner-occupiers. In other areas where property values are high and the local authority wants to prevent landlords from getting rid of sitting tenants and selling their properties for owner-occupation, it is more likely that the local authority will use its power of compulsory purchase, not least to avoid the obligation to rehouse and compensate the occupants. In such cases, however, the local authority must be careful to choose the correct procedure, since the effect of relying on one or other of the two powers provided in section 12 and section 17 respectively may be far-reaching, as illustrated in a recent test case:

Victoria Square Property Co. Ltd. v. Southwark London Borough Council (1978)
A local authority served a compulsory repair notice on the owner of an unfit house requiring him to carry out

specified works to make it fit. The owner won an appeal
in the county court on the ground that the works could
not be carried out at reasonable expense. The local
authority intended to use the power of compulsory purchase under section 12 and to carry out the works prescribed as part of a more general scheme of long-term
rehabilitation, but it omitted to ask the county court to
make an express finding that the house could not be made
fit at reasonable expense. It then attempted to use the
power of compulsory purchase under section 17. The
Court of Appeal held that this was not permissible in the
circumstances, since the local authority did not intend to
use the premises in an unimproved state on a temporary
basis, with or without minor repairs, as was envisaged in
section 17, but to carry out a long-term rehabilitation
scheme.

This means that the power of compulsory purchase under
section 17 cannot be used as a means of long-term municipalisation. Nor can a notice which prescribes works which
obviously cannot be carried out at reasonable expense be
properly served under section 9(1), since the local authority
must give some consideration to the issue (*Cohen* v. *West Ham
Corporation* (1933)) (see Appendix X). And even if the procedure under section 12 is carefully followed, the owner of the
premises may thwart compulsory purchase proceedings if the
Department of the Environment is prepared to accept a
further undertaking from him to carry out the prescribed
works (s. 12(2)). The net result is that all houses which clearly
cannot be made fit at reasonable expense should according to
the letter of the law be closed or demolished, unless the owner
is prepared to sell to the local authority on a voluntary basis.
This is one of many examples in this sphere of the essential
impracticality of the law. Local authorities which wish to
compulsorily purchase and rehabilitate unfit properties are
better advised to rely on the standard compulsory purchase
powers discussed in Chapter 8.

Compulsory repair notices for fit houses (s. 9(1A))

The paradox that local authorities had power to require

4·3 Substantial Disrepair

unfit houses to be made fit but had no power to take action to
prevent fit houses deteriorating into unfitness was highlighted by the Denington Committee in *Our Older Homes: a
call for action* (1966). The committee accordingly recommended the introduction of a new power by which local authorities
might require the owners of houses which were not unfit to
carry out specified repairs. This was provided under the
Housing Act 1969, s. 72, but is inserted as section 9(1A) of the
Housing Act 1957, if only to avoid the need to create an
entirely new set of procedures. This new power, which like
those discussed in the preceding section covers both owner-
occupied and rented houses, enables a local authority to serve
a repair notice on the person in control of any house which is in
"substantial disrepair" but is not statutorily unfit. The notice
must specify the precise works to be done and state a reasonable period for their completion as in the case of notices under
section 9(1) in respect of unfit houses.

There is no statutory guidance on what constitutes substantial disrepair, but the standard of repair which may be
required is expressly stated to be that which will bring the
house up to a reasonable standard in relation to its age,
character and locality. Any owner who objects to the terms of a
notice may then appeal to the county court, for instance on the
ground that the works prescribed are excessive or that the
house is not in substantial disrepair or that it is unfit (s. 11).
Though there is no explicit reference to the issue of reasonable
expense for notices under s. 9(1A), in contrast to those under
s. 9(1) in respect of unfit houses, the economics of the works
prescribed is often a major consideration in the proceedings on
appeal, and it has recently been decided in the Court of
Appeal that the county court judge may properly take such
matters into consideration in exercising his discretion to
confirm, vary or quash the notice (*Hillbank Properties Ltd.* v.
London Borough of Hackney) (see Appendix J). If the owner
fails either to persuade the county court that the notice should
be quashed or else to carry out the works in the period prescribed, the local authority may proceed to carry out the works
in default and collect the cost from the owner (s. 10).

This procedure is illustrated in the accompanying diagram.
It has considerable advantages in terms of relative simplicity

and the relatively short periods which may be prescribed for the completion of works. It is used in practice to deal with a wide range of forms of disrepair, frequently in the context of general rehabilitation programmes in designated areas (see Chapter 7). But its effectiveness, as with that under section 9 (1) in respect of unfit houses, depends largely on the willingness of the local authority to use its default powers. In many areas neither Environmental Health Departments nor Housing Departments are prepared to embark on substantial default works of this kind, not least because there are no effective internal structures for carrying them out. The result is often that many of the notices which are served are not enforced. Nor is there any effective method by which the tenant of a house in respect of which a notice has been served may force the local authority to pursue it. The position in this respect is even less satisfactory than in the case of notices in respect of unfit houses since the mandatory duty on local authorities to do something about all unfit houses, however unrealistic in practice, gives tenants some leverage if the matter is not pursued.

3. *Compulsory Improvement Notices under the Housing Act 1974*

Where a rented house lacks a bathroom or any other "standard amenity" there is an additional procedure by which the landlord may be required to supply them. This procedure was originally introduced under the Housing Act 1964 and is now contained in Part VIII of the Housing Act 1974. It is closely tied to the provisions for grants for the installation of standard amenities and for more comprehensive rehabilitation schemes discussed in Chapter 5, and is distinct from the procedures under the Public Health Acts and the Housing Act 1957 in that there is no need to establish any form of disrepair or unfitness. But it is convenient to deal with compulsory improvement notices in the same context as compulsory repair notices, if only because from the point of view of tenants and owners all forms of compulsory action by local authorities are inevitably grouped together.

Dwellings without standard amenities

The formal basis of the compulsory improvement procedure is the lack of standard amenities in any dwelling built before 1961. A standard amenity for this purpose is any one of the following items, currently listed under Schedule 6 of the Housing Act 1974:

    (i) a fixed bath or shower;
    (ii) a hot and cold water supply at a fixed bath or shower;
    (iii) a wash-hand basin;
    (iv) a hot and cold water supply at a wash-hand basin;
    (v) a sink;
    (vi) a hot and cold water supply at a sink;
    (vii) a water closet.

It should be noted that the lack of any of these items does not of itself render a house unfit. It should also be noted that while most of them should normally be provided in a separate bathroom, there is no strict requirement to that effect: where it is not reasonably practicable for a hot and cold water supply to a fixed bath or shower to be provided in a separate bathroom, the bath or shower may be placed anywhere other than in a bedroom. Nor is there any requirement that the water closet be provided within the dwelling, provided that it is reasonably accessible. But all the standard amenities must be provided for the exclusive use of the occupants of a single identifiable dwelling.

The requirement that compulsory improvement notices may only be served in respect of an identifiable dwelling causes no problems in respect of individual houses and self-contained flats. In rooming houses and other houses in multiple occupation, where facilities are shared by a number of households or families, it is often much less clear what constitutes a dwelling. There is certainly no requirement that a dwelling should be self-contained. But rooms or facilities shared by a number of households are probably excluded. The best test is the exclusive occupation by a single household of a sufficient number of rooms to meet all reasonable living requirements, including cooking, eating, washing and sleeping. Where a separate dwelling cannot be identified, then the separate procedures for the compulsory provision of amenities in houses in multiple occupation described in Chapter 6 must be followed. This issue is of some practical importance to tenants in that the procedure for compulsory improvement of separate dwellings extends to all kinds of repair work, while that for the provision of amenities in houses in multiple occupation does not. It is equally of importance to landlords in that the grants available for the provision of amenities in houses in multiple occupation are currently much less generous than those for separate dwellings.

What may be prescribed

The standard of work which may be prescribed in a compulsory improvement notice is identical to that for intermediate (standard amenity) grants (see Chapter 5). The maximum standard is thus whatever is necessary to ensure that when the work is completed the dwelling will have all the standard amenities, will be statutorily fit, will be in a good standard of repair in relation to its age character and locality and will have an expected life of at least fifteen years. But the total cost of the work prescribed must not exceed a reasonable expense limit similar to that laid down for compulsory repair to unfit houses. Reasonable expense for the purpose of compulsory improvement notices, however, is defined in a more general way, though it is likely to be approached by the courts in a broadly similar manner (see Appendix J). Any problems in meeting the reasonable expense criterion may in any case be eased by the fact that the local authority has a wide discretion to reduce any of the stated standards, including that of fitness, if that is necessary to keep the cost down or if it considers it reasonable to do so on any other ground, for instance the wishes of the tenant (Housing Act 1974, ss. 85(2)(a) and 89(3) (c)-(d)). The duty of local authorities to pay a full intermediate (standard amenity) grant for any works prescribed in an improvement notice further reduces the cost to the owner. The result is that virtually any scheme to provide a standard amenity along with necessary repair work may be dealt with under the compulsory improvement procedure. Though most local authorities are reluctant to reduce standards so that realistic and economically feasible improvements may be carried out, a concerted approach by the tenant and the landlord at the "time and place" meeting at which local councillors are usually present (see below) may help to induce the officials to take a more flexible approach.

Provisional and final notices

The essentials of the procedure for compulsory improvement are illustrated in the accompanying diagram. The first requirement, except in areas designated as Housing Action Areas (HAAs) or General Improvement Areas (GIAs), is a formal request by a tenant for the provision of any missing standard amenities (s. 89); the procedure is thus not available to licensees and others who are not tenants. In HAAs and GIAs the procedure may be initiated by the local authority without a formal request from anyone in respect of *any* rented dwelling but not in respect of an owner-occupied dwelling, except where satisfactory works of rehabilitation could not otherwise be carried out in an adjoining dwelling (s. 85). Even in HAAs and GIAs, however, tenants and licensees may find it useful to make a formal request to their local authority for the use of compulsory improvement powers. A suitable standard form letter of request is provided in Appendix G.

There is no obligation on a local authority to act on a tenant's request or otherwise. If it decides to do so, and is satisfied that appropriate works can be carried out at reasonable expense, the next step is the service of a provisional notice on the owner of the dwelling, on the tenant, and on any other person with a legal interest in it (s. 85(2)). This notice must include details of the works which the local authority considers to be necessary to bring the dwelling up to the required standard, and must state a time and place at which the whole matter may be discussed by all the parties. The tenant may wish, for instance, to argue that a bathroom should be provided in an existing room rather than in a newly built extension, or that an outside WC is quite sufficient or that all he wants is a fixed bath. The landlord may wish to argue that some of the prescribed works are unnecessary, or that the local authority should use its discretion to reduce the required

Compulsory Notices under the Housing Act 1974

standard of work. The landlord may also give a voluntary undertaking to carry out the required work (s. 87). If this is accepted by the local authority there is no need to proceed with the compulsory procedures.

Following the "time and place" meeting the local authority may, but need not, proceed to serve a final improvement notice on the owner or other person in control of the dwelling (ss. 88(1) and 89(5)). This notice must contain a detailed list of the prescribed works, including any amendments agreed at the "time and place" meeting, and an estimate of their cost so that the owner may have a clear idea both of the position in respect of the reasonable expense criterion and of grant aid. A period of 12 months must be prescribed for the completion of the works, except in the case of reduced standard works for which a shorter period may be allowed at the discretion of the local authority. Following the service of an improvement notice the local authority must approve any application which is made to it for an intermediate (standard amenity) grant in respect of the works prescribed (s. 67). In addition it is bound to offer a loan to cover that part of the cost which cannot be grant aided, provided that the owner can show that he can reasonably be expected to meet the repayments and interest (s. 100).

Before serving a final improvement notice the local authority must also be satisfied that the "housing arrangements" are satisfactory, *i.e.* that the occupants of the house have proper housing while the work is done and afterwards (ss. 88(2)(d) and 89(6)(b)). If a tenant agrees to move elsewhere, there must be a written agreement between him and his landlord or the local authority (s. 86(2)). The tenant may appeal if he is not satisfied about the arrangements (s. 91(3)(b)).

Appeals, purchase notices and enforcement

The person on whom a final improvement notice is served has a number of options: he may appeal to the county court to have the notice quashed; he may require the local authority to purchase the dwelling; he may carry out the works prescribed, with or without grant aid; or he may do nothing and leave it to the local authority to carry out the works in default and collect the cost.

4·4 Compulsory Improvement

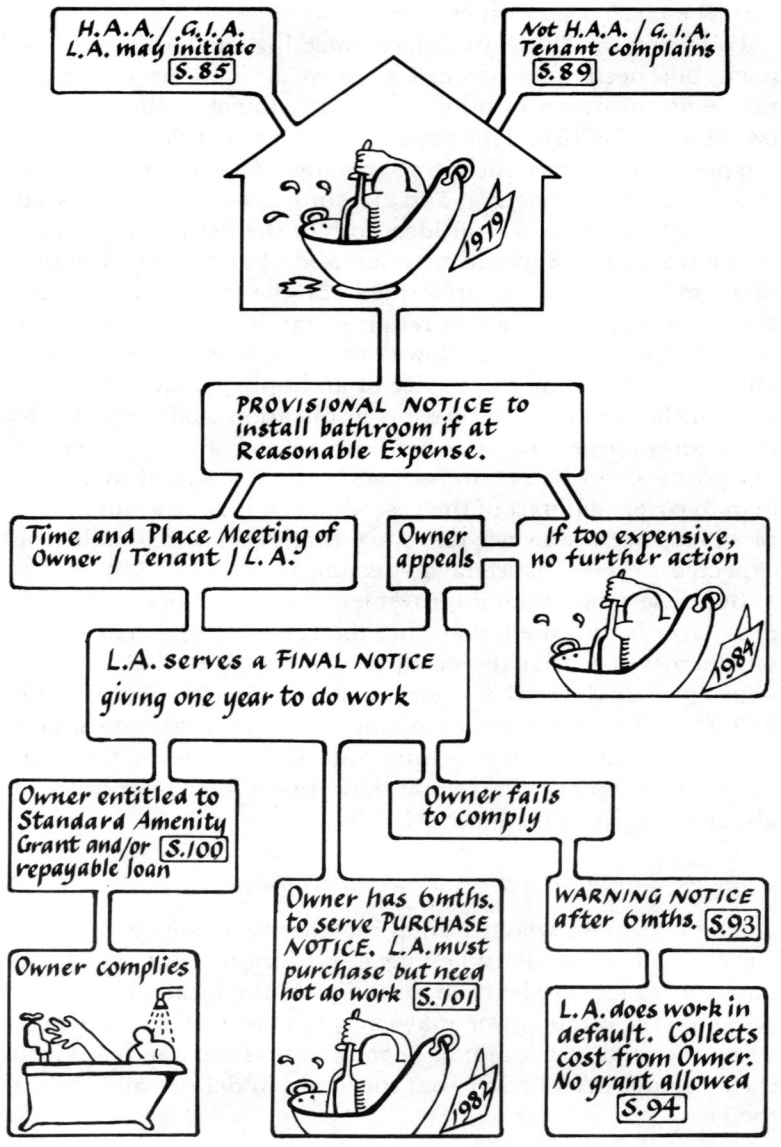

H.A.A. / G.I.A.
L.A. may initiate
S.85

Not H.A.A. / G. I. A.
Tenant complains
S.89

1979

PROVISIONAL NOTICE to
install bathroom if at
Reasonable Expense.

Time and Place Meeting of
Owner / Tenant / L. A.

Owner
appeals

If too expensive,
no further action

1984

L.A. serves a FINAL NOTICE
giving one year to do work

Owner entitled to
Standard Amenity
Grant and/or S.100
repayable loan

Owner fails
to comply

Owner has 6mths.
to serve PURCHASE
NOTICE. L.A. must
purchase but need
not do work S.101

WARNING NOTICE
after 6mths. S.93

Owner complies

1982

L.A. does work in
default. Collects
cost from Owner.
No grant allowed
S.94

The right to appeal must be exercised within six weeks (s. 91). No specific grounds are stated and the court has an unfettered discretion to confirm, vary or quash the terms of the notice. The owner may accordingly raise any of the matters discussed above in connection with the "time and place" meeting, for instance that the works prescribed are excessive, or that they cannot be carried out at reasonable expense. If the notice is confirmed it becomes immediately effective; if there is no appeal it becomes effective when the six weeks allowed for an appeal have expired (s. 92).

The owner then has a further six months in which to serve a purchase notice on the local authority (s. 101). The effect of this is that the local authority must purchase the property at a price to be fixed by agreement or by the usual procedures for settling the price under compulsory purchase orders. This right to require the local authority to purchase the property is unconditional. It is intended to give landlords who do not wish to spend money on improvement, for instance because the rate of return on such investment is too low, to obtain a fair "investment" price for their property. The local authority is then supposed to carry out the rehabilitation scheme itself, though there is no formal obligation on it to do so. In some areas tenants of dwellings in respect of which purchase notices have been served have had to wait months and even years before anything is done by the local authority to improve conditions, despite the fact that the local authority has the right to take possession of the dwelling immediately the purchase notice is served (s. 101(2) and Compulsory Purchase Act 1965, s. 11).

If the owner neither serves a purchase notice nor shows any serious intention of carrying out the prescribed works, for instance by applying for a grant and submitting tenders, the local authority may proceed to enforcement. When the time limit for the service of a purchase notice expires, the local authority may serve a formal reminder on the owner asking whether he intends to carry out the works (s. 93(3)). If this does not produce a satisfactory response, the local authority may serve a further notice stating that it intends to carry out the works in default, and after a further 21 days it may proceed to do so (s. 93(4)). Alternatively it may wait until the full 12

months allowed in the notice have expired and then act in
default, though it must still give the owner 21 days notice of its
intention to do so. In either case the cost of the works may then
be recovered from the owner, subject to any further appeal by
the owner against the amount claimed (s. 94).

The procedure in practice

The administration of this procedure is sometimes entrusted
to the Environmental Health Department, sometimes to the
Housing Department, and sometimes to the section in either
department which deals with grants. It has never been exten-
sively used. The initial statutory provisions under the Housing
Act 1964 were widely criticised in local government circles in
that works of repair could not be prescribed unless they were
essential to permit the installation of standard amenities.
Under the Housing Act 1974 substantial works of repair and
renewal unrelated to the provision of missing amenities may
now be prescribed, and may also be grant aided provided they
do not exceed 50 per cent of the total cost (see Chapter 5). But
the results have not been particularly encouraging. In the
period from January 1975 to March 1977 a total of some 4,500
improvement notices were served throughout England and
Wales; works were completed in fewer than one third of the
cases; yet local authorities used their default powers in less
than one hundred cases (T. Hadden, *Compulsory Repair and
Improvement* (1978) p. 38). This pattern appears to be due
partly to the extended time-scales which are laid down for
enforcement, partly to the reluctance of local authorities to
prescribe works to a reduced standard, partly to their reluctance to use their default powers, and partly to the policies
adopted in HAAs (see Chapter 7).

The compulsory improvement procedure is nonetheless a
useful addition to the powers under the Housing Act 1957 and
the Public Health Acts from the point of view of tenants living
in unsatisfactory conditions. Provided that a separate dwelling
can be identified, whether in a separate house or flat or within
a house in multiple occupation, and that at least one standard
amenity is lacking, tenants who are prepared to take the
initiative in asking for compulsory improvement and to put

pressure on their local authorities to use their powers of enforcement may achieve a substantial improvement in their living conditions.

4. *Special Procedures for Listed Buildings*

Brief mention should also be made of the special procedures for the protection and compulsory repair of buildings officially listed as of historic or architectural interest. If such buildings are occupied the standard procedures under the Public Health and Housing Acts may be applied in the usual way. If they are unoccupied and thus arguably not dwelling-houses, these procedures may not be applicable. Additional powers have accordingly been provided under the Town and Country Planning Act 1971 to permit local authorities to prevent owners from allowing such houses to fall into irretrievable disrepair, often with a view to securing their demolition and the more profitable use of the site.

In the first place local authorities may serve a repair notice on the owner of any listed building requiring him to carry out any specified works necessary to the preservation of the building (s. 115). If the owner fails to comply with such a notice within two months, the local authority may then institute compulsory purchase proceedings on the sole ground that the building is in need of repair (s. 114). Where it can be shown that the owner has deliberately left the building derelict, the local authority need only pay what is termed minimum compensation, that is current market value without any addition in respect of development value (s. 117). In urgent cases the local authority may also after serving seven days notice on the owner carry out any works urgently required for the preservation of an unoccupied listed building and collect the cost from the owner (s. 101, as substituted by the Town and Country Amenities Act 1974). And to deter owners from demolishing listed buildings it is further provided that it is an offence to demolish or substantially alter the character of a listed building without what is termed a "listed building consent" from the Department of the Environment or the local planning authority. These protections may be extended to specific unlisted buildings by means of a temporary building

preservation order (s. 58) and to buildings in Conservation
Areas under the Town and Country Amenities Act 1974.

These powers have not been widely used, not least because
many local authorities appear to be as reluctant as many
owners to take on the renovation or maintenance of listed
buildings. Under the Housing Act 1974 additional provisions
were introduced to prevent local authorities themselves from
demolishing listed buildings in clearance areas (ss. 110-112).
The major difficulty is that the additional grant aid provided
for the repair and rehabilitation of listed buildings is grossly
inadequate given the very substantial costs which must often
be incurred (see Chapter 5).

5. *The Choice of Procedures*

It is clear from this account of each of the separate procedures
under the Public Health and Housing Acts that there is a good
deal of overlap between them. In many cases the local
authority will have a choice between serving a notice for the
abatement of a statutory nuisance and serving a compulsory
repair notice under section 9(1) or section 9(1A) of the
Housing Act 1957 and in the case of tenanted premises a compulsory improvement notice under the Housing Act 1974.
Tenants themselves, in addition to their right to enforce the
terms of their tenancy agreement, may rely on section 99 of the
Public Health Act 1936 to secure the abatement of a statutory
nuisance, and if they can show that their dwelling is unfit may
in theory, if not in practice, require the local authority either
to have it made fit or else rehouse them. The object of this
final section is to set out some of the advantages and disadvantages of the various alternatives from the points of view
of local authorities, owners and tenants, and to give some
practical guidance to tenants and other occupiers on their best
course of action in particular circumstances. Before this can be
attempted, however, a brief account must also be given of the
formal legal interrelationship between the statutory nuisance
and unfitness procedures.

The interrelationship between the Public Health and Housing Acts

The strict statutory position is that the powers and duties imposed under the Housing Acts are entirely independent of those imposed under the Public Health Acts. It is expressly provided that the service of compulsory repair notices under the Housing Act 1957 shall not "prejudice or affect any other powers of the local authority, or any remedy available to the tenant of a house, either at common law or otherwise" (s. 10 (9)). Thus abatement notices and orders under the Public Health Acts may be served in respect of premises which have already been declared unfit and are awaiting closure or demolition or rehabilitation, or in respect of which compulsory repair or improvement notices are outstanding. This was clearly established in a test case in which the occupier of an unfit house in a clearance area, which had been retained in use by the local authority on a "temporary" basis, obtained an abatement order against the local authority under the Public Health Act 1936, s. 99:

> *Salford City Council v. McNally (1975)*
> The tenant of a house in a clearance area made a complaint to the magistrates court in respect of general disrepair. The house had already been declared to be unfit some years previously and had been compulsorily purchased with a view to demolition. But the local authority had exercised its power to retain it in use on a temporary basis under the Housing Act 1957, s. 48. The magistrates held that the conditions in the house constituted a statutory nuisance and ordered the local authority to abate it. The local authority appealed on the ground that they had statutory authority to use the house in an unfit condition. It was held in the House of Lords that since the procedures under the Public Health Acts were entirely independent from those under the Housing Acts the magistrates had been correct in ordering the local authority to abate the nuisance.

This means that anyone occupying a house which is unfit or in poor condition may obtain some assistance under the Public Health Acts, regardless of whether demolition or rehabilitation is planned or pending, though the magistrates may exercise their discretion to postpone any order for a period of some months if that seems reasonable in all the circumstances (*Nottingham District Council* v. *Newton* (1974) (see above). The net result, however, may well be to precipitate the closure or demolition of the house, as happened in Mrs McNally's case, rather than the completion of the works prescribed to abate the nuisance.

It does not follow from this that orders made under the Public Health Acts will always prevail over those made under the Housing Acts. There are circumstances in which owners or landlords may rely on the duty of local authorities to take action in respect of unfit houses as a means of countering a notice served on them under the Public Health Acts. The operation of an abatement notice may thus be postponed until the local authority has complied with its duty under the Housing Acts:

R. v. *Kerrier District Council, ex. p. Guppys*
(*Bridport*) *Ltd* (*1976*)

The landlord of two unfit cottages wished to get rid of a sitting tenant and combine the two cottages into a single dwelling. The local authority served a notice on him under the Public Health Act 1936 requiring him to carry out specified works in the occupied cottage. The landlord appealed on the ground that since the houses were unfit and could not be made fit at reasonable cost, the local authority should have made a closing order and rehoused the sitting tenant. This argument was upheld in the Court of Appeal which sent the case back to the local authority with an instruction that the case under the Public Health Act should be adjourned until the local authority had established whether the house could be made fit at reasonable expense; if it could not, then the local authoirty had a statutory duty to close it and rehouse the tenant.

This decision does not mean that in such cases landlords may succeed in forcing the local authority to rehouse sitting tenants, thus permitting a sale at a greatly enhanced price, since the local authority may if it wishes exercise its powers of compulsory purchase (see above). But it makes it clear that the decision in *Salford City Council* v. *McNally* is limited in respect of unfit houses to those cases in which the local authority has used its statutory powers to retain unfit houses in use for the time being.

These two examples do not exhaust the possibilities of overlap or conflict between the various procedures, though they are perhaps those most likely to be met with in practice. But the approach of the courts is likely to be similar in other such cases. Where there is potential conflict between the orders which may have to be made as a result of concurrent proceedings, one or other of them will simply be adjourned until a legally satisfactory solution or compromise is reached.

The procedures compared

In comparing the relative advantages and disadvantages of the procedures under the Public Health and Housing Acts it is essential to distinguish the different interests of local authorities, owners and tenants. Local authorities are typically concerned to ensure that public money is spent on securing the highest possible standards of repair and improvement, though political commitments to owner-occupation or to municipalisation often take effective precedence. Landlords are typically most concerned to maintain a reasonable net income from their properties. Owner-occupiers are often concerned to maintain property values in their area. And tenants are usually concerned to achieve the highest possible standards of maintenance and repair at minimum cost to themselves. Since no legal structure can possibly satisfy all these demands at once, some element of compromise is inevitable. The proper question is not whether the existing procedures fully satisfy the demands of any one interest, but whether an acceptable balance has been struck.

The particular advantages of the procedures for the enforcement of statutory or contractual covenants from the point of view of tenants are that responsibility is clearly placed on the landlord, that there is no test of reasonable expense, and that since 1974 there has been a reasonably effective method of enforcement by an action in the county court for specific performance. The disadvantages are that the tenant or his advisers must bear the full burden, both psychologically and administratively, of initiating and carrying through the action and that only tenants, as opposed to licensees and other occupiers, may sue. The corresponding advantage of the statutory nuisance procedures is that the administrative burden can be left to the local authority, except in cases where council tenants and others may have to fall back on their right to take their own proceedings under section 99. The principal drawback of relying on the abatement of a statutory nuisance as opposed to the enforcement of a statutory or contractual covenant is that the extent of the work which may be required is much less extensive: the statutory covenants cover any failure to maintain most essential fixtures and fittings as well as structural and external disrepair, many of which might not readily be accepted by the local authority or by the magistrates as constituting a statutory nuisance. Neither procedure permits the tenant to insist on any *improvement* in conditions or in the supply of amenities or facilities. If action of this kind is required, then he must fall back on the discretionary application of the procedures under the Housing Acts by the local authority. If his house is clearly unfit, then by drawing attention to this fact, for instance by submitting a surveyor's report on the general state of the premises and the facilities provided, he may put pressure on the local authority to take some action. But the end result may be closure and rehousing in scarcely more satisfactory conditions or even a compulsory purchase by the local authority which may then do nothing either to improve conditions or to rehouse the occupants for long periods. The unfitness strategy should be relied on only after careful consideration of the policy which the local authority is likely to adopt in fulfilling its obligations to rehouse displaced occupants (see Chapter 8) or in carrying out its own schemes of rehabilitation.

From the point of view of local authorities, the principal choice is between reliance on repair notices under the Public Health Acts and the Housing Act 1957, on compulsory improvement-notices or on compulsory purchase followed by rehabilitation or renewal by the local authority itself or an approved housing association. For reasons of departmental organisation and tradition many local authorities have relied primarily on the Public Health Act procedures, dealt with by Environmental Health Departments, for private sector properties and on the Housing Act procedures for clearance, renewal and rehabilitation, dealt with primarily by Housing Departments. There is a general belief that the enforcement procedures for abatement notices under the Public Health Acts are superior to those under the Housing Acts, and much larger numbers of the former are typically served. From an objective legal point of view there is little to support this view, since in either case the ultimate sanction is the carrying out of the works in default by the local authority. But the fact that court proceedings with the sanction of fines and costs are available under the Public Health Acts but not under the Housing Acts is an important consideration in areas where there is any reluctance to resort to default action. Except in the case of compulsory improvement notices there is no effective difference in the time scales which may be prescribed for the completion of works under the Public Health and Housing Acts. Another major procedural consideration is that compulsory repair notices for unfit houses under the Housing Act 1957, s. 9(1) and compulsory improvement notices under the Housing Act 1974 are governed by the reasonable expense criterion, while those under the Public Health Acts and the Housing Act 1957, s. 9(1A) in respect of fit houses are not. This is in itself an important reason for adopting a more stringent standard for the designation of houses as unfit, in addition to the risk that unfit houses may have to be closed and the occupants rehoused and compensated.,

A more important consideration in many areas is the standard of works which may be prescribed. Under the Public Health Acts, as has been seen, only essential works of repair can be prescribed. Under the Housing Act 1957 owners may be required to undertake more comprehensive rehabilitation either to render the house fit or if the house is not deemed to be unfit to bring it up to a good standard of repair. In practice there is unlikely to be much difference between these two standards. But neither permits the local authority to insist on the provision of the full range of standard amenities nor on proper electrical or heating facilities or insulation. To achieve a substantial improvement in conditions the local authority must

rely on compulsory improvement procedures under the
Housing Act 1974 or on their powers to make discretionary
grants for full standard improvement and conversion. Compulsory improvement notices, however, may not include the
provision of facilities for heating or the installation of electricity, though where the house is already wired, works necessary to electrical safety, including rewiring, are widely prescribed on the ground that this is essential to achieve a reasonable standard of repair. Many local authorities accordingly
prefer to use the service of compulsory repair and improvement notices as a means of inducing owners to apply for
discretionary grants or to sell their properties to the local
authority or a housing association so that more comprehensive
rehabilitation may be prescribed (see further Chapters 5 and
7). There is continuing argument within local authorities and
on a more general political level on whether it is better to
achieve the rehabilitation of fewer houses to this very high
standard by persuasion or municipalisation or to use the
procedures for compulsory repair and improvement to a lower
standard in more houses.

Practical guidance for tenants

It is impossible to lay down any precise rules for the choice of
procedures, given the wide range of interlocking considerations. But the following guidelines may be of assistance in
more straightforward cases.

The most satisfactory procedure, where it is available, is
probably the enforcement of the statutory covenants under the
Housing Act 1961, s. 32 (see Chapter 3). This is available to all
tenants, but not licensees and others, whose tenancy was
granted before October 1, 1961. For this purpose it is the date
of occupation as tenant rather than any changes in rent or
conditions which constitutes the granting of a tenancy. Both
council tenants and private sector tenants are covered, and
both may rely either on a county court action or in appropriate
cases on the self-help remedy of doing the repairs themselves
and deducting the cost from the rent provided the procedures
stipulated in Chapter 3 are carefully followed.

Where the statutory covenants under the Housing Act 1961

do not apply, it may be possible to rely on the statutory covenant of fitness under the Housing Act 1957, s. 6, provided that the rent for the tenancy, including rates, is less than £52 per year on contracts made after 1957 (in London £80); less than £26 on those made before 1957 in towns of more than 50,000 (in London £40); and in smaller towns less than £26 on those made between 1923 and 1957 or less than £16 on those made before 1923. But a new contract is probably made every time the rent is changed, so that few tenants other than those whose rent has long been controlled (not regulated) will now be covered.

Where there is no protection under these statutory covenants or equivalent contractual provisions in the tenancy agreement, it is probably best to rely on the procedures for the abatement of statutory nuisances under the Public Health Acts. Private sector tenants may even prefer this method to the enforcement of covenants since the burden of initiating and carrying through the procedures falls on the Environmental Health Department. But council tenants and some others may have to rely on the right of individual complaint to the magistrates court under the Public Health Act 1936, s. 99 which is not in practice any simpler than taking action in a county court to enforce a covenant.

Where a tenant lacks a standard amenity, he may also make a formal application for the implementation of the compulsory improvement procedures under the Housing Act 1974. The right to make representations for this purpose, however, is restricted to those tenants who are not in HAAs or GIAs and gives no guarantee that the local authority will proceed to serve and enforce a notice. Even if it does, the end result may well be a compulsory or voluntary purchase by the local authority.

Finally where a tenant or any other lawful occupant of a house which is demonstrably unfit is prepared to or wishes to be moved elsewhere at the discretion of the local authority Housing Department he may seek to enforce the local authority's duty to ensure that every unfit house is either closed or else made fit. The danger is that the tenant thereby loses any security of tenure he may have and that in the case of privately rented houses the local authority may simply compulsory purchase the property and maintain it in use on a "temporary" basis for an indefinite period.

Further Reading

The best accounts of the practical operation of the various procedures covered in this chapter are to be found in the series of Practice Notes prepared by Philag's Public Health Advisory Service Ltd., currently obtainable from Publications Distribution Co-op, 27 Clerkenwell Close, London EC1: for a more general survey from the same source see David Ormandy, *Guide to Public Health and Housing Law* (2nd edition) (1977); for a more technical account by the same author see the section on "Housing: Public Health" in D.W. Pollard (ed.), *Social Welfare Law* (1977); the standard practitioners' works also widely used by local authority officers, are the *Encyclopedia of Public Health* (recently renamed *Encyclopedia of Environmental Health Law and Practice*) and the *Encyclopedia of Housing Law and Practice* which are voluminous and not always easy to digest but contain all relevant statutes, statutory instruments and circulars; for a detailed discussion of the statutory nuisance procedure see D. Hughes, "Public Health Legislation and the Improvement of Housing Conditions" and "What is a Nuisance?," (1976) 27 N.I.L.Q. 1 and 131; for a more general discussion of the interrelationship of the public health and housing codes see T. Hadden, "Public Health and Housing Legislation: Towards an Integrated Code of Procedure," (1976) N.I.L.Q. 245; for a description of current local authority practice see T. Hadden, *Compulsory Repair and Improvement*, Centre for Socio-Legal Studies, Wolfson College, Oxford, Research Study No. 1 (1978); for current cases see the LAG Bulletin and the *Journal of Social Welfare Law.*

5 Grants

The provision of grants towards the repair and improvement
of older houses is the central element of the current rehabilitation strategy. Grants are available for all sectors, including
privately rented housing, and may be taken up either voluntarily or following the service of compulsory repair or improvement notices. Four distinct types of grant are currently
provided for under the Housing Act 1974, Part VII:
> (i) *intermediate grants* for the provision of standard
> amenities and associated repairs;
> (ii) *improvement grants* for the general rehabilitation of
> separate dwellings or for the conversion of large
> houses into separate flats or dwellings;
> (iii) *repairs grants* for the repair of houses in HAAs and
> GIAs;
> (iv) *special grants* for the provision of facilities in houses
> in multiple occupation.
A fifth type, *home insulation grants*, was introduced in 1978.
In addition there are certain other provisions for the funding
of works in buildings which are listed as being of particular
architectural or historic merit, whether individually or in
groups. The detailed rules which govern the administration of
each of these types of grant will be discussed in turn. But since
all grants are dealt with in a broadly similar way, certain
general principles of law and practice will be introduced at the
outset.

1. *The General Principles of Grant Aid*

Proportional contribution

The first basic principle of the grant system is that owners
should be paid only a proportion of the total cost of the work

which is necessary to bring their dwellings up to the relevant standard. The basic proportion prescribed under the Housing Act 1974 for most purposes is one half (s. 59). Higher proportions are offered in areas specially designated for rehabilitation to give greater encouragement to owners: in General Improvement Areas (GIAs) the standard proportion is 60 per cent; in Housing Action Areas (HAAs) it is 75 per cent, and in cases where the applicant cannot finance his contribution to the works without undue hardship 90 per cent (s. 59). The notes of guidance issued by the Department of the Environment on the interpretation of "undue hardship" suggest that local authorities should look at each case on its merits and give favourable consideration to any applicant who is dependent on supplementary benefit or a state pension or who is entitled to a rate rebate; but it is assumed that all applicants will normally be expected to submit to a means test (Circular 160/74, Appendix B, Paras. 4-5). Practice in this respect varies widely from area to area: some authorities have developed elaborate methods of calculating the amount which owner-occupiers or landlords might be expected to contribute to grant-aided improvement; others apply much less precise criteria (see E. Monck, *Grants and Hardship Allowances in HAAs*, CES Working Note 439, 1976). Whether or not undue hardship can be established, however, many local authorities offer loans to cover the balance of the cost of approved works for which grant aid is not payable. Such loans may be granted on a maturity basis, under which the applicant pays only interest until his property is sold, to elderly or impecunious applicants.

A simple example may help to clarify the way the system works. If the total cost of the works approved by the local authority is £1,000, the applicant for a grant would be paid £750 (or £900 in cases of special need) if his dwelling is in an HAA, £600 if it is in a GIA and £500 if it is not in an HAA or a GIA. In each case he would have to provide the rest himself, or else take up a loan from the local authority or his building society or his bank for the remainder, and pay it off over a longer period. The idea behind this system is that owners should be expected to make some contribution to improving conditions in their own houses. The real or psychological difficulties which elderly people and low income households face in raising or paying off their contributions, however, has contributed to a relatively low uptake of grants in certain areas, and there is some pressure on the government to agree to make 100% grants in appropriate cases.

Maximum expenditure limits

There is in addition a maximum permitted amount in respect of each type of grant on which the appropriate proportional grant may be based. The purpose of these limits is to impose some control on the expenditure of local authorities in this sphere, since most of the ultimate cost is borne by central government. The current maximum expenditure limits for each type of grant, prescribed in August 1977, are set out in Table 5.1. It should be noted that these figures are increased from time to time. It may on occasions be an advantage to delay an application if an increase is in the pipeline, since it is the date of the application rather than its approval which governs the amount which may be paid. It should also be noted that local authorities may insist on works which cost more than the maximum permitted limit. This means that owners may be expected to contribute more than the appropriate percentage. Thus, for instance, if a local authority required an owner in a GIA to carry out works costing £6,000 as a condition of approving an improvement grant the effective percentage contribution from the owner would work out at 50 per cent, since the maximum grant payable would be 60 per cent of the permitted maximum of £5,000, *i.e.* £3,000.

Repairs and improvements

The computation of the effective contribution of owners is further complicated by statutory restrictions on the amount of any grant which may be allocated to repairs as opposed to improvements. The current maximum repair element varies from £1,500 to £2,900, as set out in Table 5.1, and is fixed in different ways for intermediate grants (for which separate maximum figures are prescribed for repairs and improvements) and for improvement and conversion grants (for which the maximum repair element is set at half the total (s. 63(2)). Thus if an owner in a GIA applied for an intermediate grant

Table 5.1
The maximum expenditure limits for the various types
of grant and the appropriate proportions payable to
applicants in HAAs, GIAs and elsewhere

Maximum permitted expenditure

Type of grant	Improvement element	Repair element	Total
Intermediate grant (standard amenities)	£1,200	£1,500	£2,700
Improvement grant	£5,000	£2,500	£5,000
Conversion grant for houses of three or more storeys (per unit)	£5,800	£2,900	£5,800
Repairs grant		£1,500	£1,500
Special grant (facilities in HMOs)	Fixed sum per item		No limit

Appropriate percentages

Housing Action Areas	75%
Housing Action Areas (cases of hardship)	90%
General Improvement Areas	60%
Elsewhere	50%

Source: S.I. 2066 (August 1977)

for which the improvement element was costed at £1,000 and the repair element at £1,500, the applicant would be paid 60 per cent of £1,000 plus £1,500, *i.e.* £1,500, and would be expected to contribute £1,000 himself. But if the same owner applied for an improvement grant for the same works, he would be paid only 60 per cent of £1,000 plus £1,000, *i.e.* £1,200, since £500 of the repair works would have to be disallowed to bring the repair element down to half the total. To give another example, if an owner in a non-designated area applied for an improvement grant for which the local authority insisted on works of improvement costed at £3,500 and works of repair costed at £4,000, he would be paid 50 per cent of £3,500 plus £1,500, *i.e.* £2,500, since the remainder of the repair works would have to be disallowed on the ground that they brought the total above the maximum of £5,000. The result is that owners are expected to contribute a highly variable amount depending on the type of grant, the standard of work required, the balance between repairs and improvements and the designation of the area in which the house is situated.

It will be clear from these examples that the classification of items of work as repairs or improvements may make a substantial difference to the amount of grant which may be payable, and that when a high standard of work is prescribed it will often be to the advantage of the applicant to have as many items as possible treated as improvements rather than as repairs. There are no statutory guidelines for this purpose and practice varies widely from area to area. Certain items, such as the building of a new bathroom or kitchen extension can only be classed as improvements, and some others only as repairs, such as the replacement of rotting timberwork. But it is often possible to argue that items like the replacement of a whole window or the replastering of a wall constitute improvements if the end result is even slightly better or different from what was there originally. The allocation of items is carried out by local authority officials while processing the grant application, but there is no reason why individual applicants should not put a case for the reclassification of certain items if that would increase the amount of grant payable. A schedule of items which are treated as improvements by a number of local authorities in London, based on a survey carried out by the Consumers' Association in 1976, is set out in Appendix H.

Local authority discretion

The second general principle of the grant system is that local authorities should themselves decide whether to approve applications for grants and what standard of work to prescribe. There are some fixed statutory requirements for each type of grant, as discussed below, and local authorities are bound to approve eligible applications for intermediate (standard amenity) grants. Apart from this each local authority is free to develop its own policy. Since most authorities approve eligible applications for improvement and conversion grants more or less as a matter of course, the most important aspects of local authority discretion in practical terms is their approach to repairs and special grants, and the more general issue of the standard of work to be prescribed for all grant aided work. The Housing Act 1974 provides a general framework for the standards to be applied for each type of grant. But local authorities have a wide discretion to waive or reduce particular requirements. There are accordingly what are called "full standard" and "reduced standard" works for each type of grant. Most local authorities take the view that full standard works should be prescribed wherever possible. But most are prepared to consider making a specific reduction if a strong case is made out by an individual applicant.

The flexibility of the system is further increased by the fact that the statutory guidelines on full standard works are framed in very general terms. There is accordingly a similar lack of clarity on what precise works may properly be prescribed as on the difference between repairs and improvements. In some areas grant inspectors prescribe expensive materials and fittings for all grant aided works, for instance the tiling of bathrooms and the provision of cabinets in kitchens. In others such items may be disallowed for grant purposes as unnecessarily expensive, with the result that the applicant himself will have to pay the full cost if they are installed. There is also considerable flexibility on repairs. Local authorities have been advised that for the purpose of improvement grants all repairs that would be likely to become necessary within a few years of the improvement, such as reroofing, rewiring or the replacement of defective guttering, should be prescribed (Circular 180/74, Appendix B, para. 26). But this does *not* mean that everything in the dwelling must have an estimated life of 30 years. The difficulty is that the discretion given to local authorities to approve or reject grant applications permits them to insist on unrealistically high standards as a condition of approving any grant at all. This extends even to prescribing works in excess of the statutory full standard.

From the point of view of individual applicants the effect of an insistence on the highest standards by local authority officials will depend on whether the maximum permitted expenditure is exceeded. If it is not then there is some advantage in having a high standard of work prescribed, since all such work will qualify for the relevant proportional grant. But if the limit is exceeded, the applicant will have to bear the full cost of all excess items. As on most issues concerning grants, the applicant has no formal right of appeal against local authority decisions. But if the matter is openly discussed, some form of compromise may often be reached. In any event it is important to find out what approach is likely to be adopted before issuing instructions to contractors.

Making an application

There is little uniformity over the allocation of responsibility for grants within local authorities. In most areas applications must be made to a section within the Environmental Health or Housing Department; in some others grants are administered by the Architect's or Surveyor's Department. Once the correct department has been located, however, the procedure is straightforward. The applicant will be asked to fill in an initial form for the relevant grant, giving details of the age and ownership of the property and a broad indication of the works envisaged. The next step is likely to be a visit to the house by a grant inspector, who will prepare a schedule of works which the local authority considers necessary. The applicant will then be expected to obtain a contractor's estimate or tender for the works and to submit this, together with appropriate plans, for formal consideration by the relevant committee or official within the local authority. It may also be necessary to obtain the consent of the Planning Department and of the Buildings Inspectors for the proposed works. All this may be left to the applicant himself or to his contractor. In some more progressive areas, however, the local authority itself undertakes to carry out all the necessary formalities, including the preparation of plans, obtaining tenders and supervising the works: in Birmingham, for instance, a comprehensive "House Improvement Service" is offered for a flat fee of £25, and in the London Borough of Brent a free service is offered to a limited number of applicants in HAAs and GIAs who might not otherwise be able to pursue an application. In other areas a list of suitable contractors, who are prepared to undertake grant works and who normally undertake to deal with all the paper-work, is maintained by the local authority. There is a strict rule in all cases that no work shall begin until the application has been formally approved. It is particularly important to see that this rule is adhered to in cases where the work is to be carried out by small jobbing builders or by the applicant himself. The progress of the works will then be supervised by local authority officials to ensure that proper standards are maintained. When the contract has been completed, a final certificate will be issued. Payment of the grant is not normally made until this certificate has been issued, but where substantial works are involved it may be possible to obtain some payment on account for work which has been satisfactorily completed.

The time which all this will take depends largely on the efficiency of the local authority grants section. In a well organised area the processing of the application from the initial approach to final approval should not take more than six or eight weeks, so that work should be started within about three months. In many areas, however, the processing of the application may take up to six months or more. The delay is not always caused within the grants section itself. Approval of the plans may be held up by those concerned with planning or building regulations consents, and any application for a loan may have to await formal confirmation from the Finance Department. But the fact that much shorter time limits are adhered to in many authorities suggests that there may be legitimate cause for complaint if a straightforward application is not dealt with in less than three months.

Possible repayment

There is a risk in certain circumstances that the whole or part of any grant other than a special grant may have to be refunded by the applicant. Local authorities are required to obtain from all applicants a certificate that the dwelling for which the grant is given will either be used for owner-occupation or will be available for letting for a period of five years from the completion of the grant-aided works (s. 60). For dwellings in HAAs the period of availability for letting is extended to seven years (s. 75(4)). Landlords may be, and in HAAs must be, required to give certain other covenants for the protection of their tenants (s. 74). If an owner-occupier or a landlord breaches such an undertaking, he may be required to refund all or part of the grant which he has received with interest though local authorities may waive the requirement if they think fit (s. 76). Even the prospect of having to repay any grant, however, has deterred some potential applicants in areas where the increase in property values following rehabilitation is less than the owner's contribution. The Department of the Environment has accordingly advised local authorities to waive repayment in any case in which owner-occupiers are forced to sell their houses to take up employment elsewhere or for other good reasons (Circular 38/77). In practical terms repayment is likely to be required only from landlords who seek to sell improved properties within the five or seven year period. From the point of view of owner-occupiers the main impact of the requirement to give a certificate of owner-occupation is to prevent grants being made for second houses, since the certificate covers continued occupation as the only or main residence of the applicant and members of his household (s. 60(3)).

2. *Intermediate (Standard Amenity) Grants*

Grants for the installation of standard amenities were the first to be introduced and have always been treated differently from other grants. Initially the grant was payable only in respect of the cost of installing the amenities themselves. Now under the Housing Act 1974 additional payments may be made for repair work quite unrelated to the provision of amenities (s. 68). The maximum permitted expenditure for each missing standard amenity, however, is still fixed at a precise amount. The current provision is as follows:

A fixed bath or shower	£180
A hot and cold water supply at a fixed bath or shower	£230
A wash-hand- basin	£ 70
A hot and cold water supply at a wash-hand basin	£120

A sink	£180
A hot and cold water supply at a sink	£150
A water closet	£270
Repairs and renewals	£1,500

As with other grants only the relevant proportions of these amounts, *i.e.* 75 per cent or 90 per cent in HAAs, 60 per cent in GIAs and 50 per cent elsewhere are payable to the applicant. But if the applicant is eligible, the local authority is bound to approve the application (s. 67(1)); and if a compulsory improvement notice has been served (see Chapter 4), grant-aid must be approved for all the works prescribed in the notice (s. 67(2)).

Eligibility

The provisions for eligibility are quite straightforward. The applicant must be either an owner-occupier, a landlord or a tenant under a fixed term tenancy which has at least five years to run (s. 57(3)). In the case of owner-occupiers a certificate of owner-occupation for a period of five years and in the case of a landlord a certificate of availability for letting for a period of five years (in HAAs seven years) must be given (ss. 60 and 75 (4)). The dwelling must have been without at least one of the listed amenities for a period of at least one year, unless the existing amenities are inaccessible to a registered disabled person (s. 65(3)). It must have been built, or in the case of converted dwellings converted, before October 2 1961 (s. 56 (3) and Circular 160/74, paras. 2-3). There are no limits in respect of the rateable value of the dwelling.

Full and reduced standards

Works to the full standard for the purposes of an intermediate grant are such as when completed will ensure:
    (i) that the dwelling will be statutorily fit;
    (ii) that its occupants will have exclusive, but not necessarily self-contained, use of all standard amenities;
    (iii) that it will be properly insulated;
    (iv) that it will be in good repair in relation to its age, character and locality;

(v) that it is likely to have fifteen years of future use as a dwelling.

Until 1978 the prescribed standard for proper insulation was such as would meet current Building Regulations, Part F, which require that roof spaces should have a thermal transfer coefficient equivalent to 50mm of insulation material, but grant aid in respect of insulation was permitted only in the case of elderly or disabled applicants (Circular 160/74, Appendix A). Under the Home Insulation Scheme 1978 grant aid is now generally available for insulation (see below). The required standard has therefore been increased to the higher level of insulation required under the scheme (Circular 60/78, Appendix E).

Any of these requirements, however, may be waived at the discretion of the local authority if it is satisfied that works to the full standard could not be carried out at reasonable expense (s. 66(3)-(4)), or that it would be reasonable to set an expected future use of less than fifteen years (s. 66(5)). It has been argued that it cannot be lawful to waive the requirement that on the completion of the works the dwelling should be statutorily fit, given the mandatory nature of the obligation to deal with all unfit houses under the Housing Act 1957. But since the Housing Act 1974 is quite explicit on the right of local authorities to waive the requirement of fitness, the better view is that grant aid may be given for the installation of standard amenities and for associated repairs in an unfit dwelling, at least on a temporary basis.

Applicants for an intermediate grant cannot require their local authority to reduce the statutory full standard. Since eligible applications must be approved, however, they may resist any attempt by their local authority to insist on more than the full standard. The main issue in this context is likely to be the location of the amenities. As in the case of compulsory improvement notices (see Chapter 4), there is no requirement that the W.C., the bathroom or the kitchen shall be provided within a self-contained dwelling. In converted houses it is perfectly proper for such facilities to be provided across a corridor, in the "return" or even on another floor. Applicants may also rely on the provision that the full standard may be reduced in cases where it cannot be attained at reasonable

expense. There is no formal statutory definition of reasonable
expense for this purpose. But applicants may well rely on the
criteria developed for the purposes of compulsory improvement notices (see Appendix J). In particular it may be argued
that attainment of the requisite standard of repair does not
require the *renewal* of all defective woodwork or guttering or
pointing, but merely such repair as is necessary to make it
efficient, safe or weatherproof. There is no need for the repairs
to last the full fifteen year period, since the requirement in this
respect is merely that the dwelling is likely to be available as a
dwelling for that period, which is primarily a matter of
planning. Applicants who are dissatisfied with the approach of
local authority officials on any of these matters may usefully
make representations to their local councillors.

Until the 1970s grants for the provision of standard amenities were much more frequently approved than improvement
grants. Though the number of intermediate grants has now
dropped from an average of some 50,000 per year to less than
10,000, an intermediate grant may still be the most satisfactory alternative in cases where owners would have difficulty
in meeting the full cost of their contribution to an improvement grant for works to the standard which many local
authorities insist upon.

3. *Improvement Grants*

Improvement grants for the rehabilitation of single houses and
the conversion of larger houses into separate dwellings are now
the most widely used type of grant. Since the levels of grant
were increased in 1969, the number of these discretionary
grants has been running at an average of some 100,000 per
year for the private sector, despite a sharp fall following the
public expenditure cuts of 1974 and 1975. Under the Housing
Act 1974 amounts of from 50 per cent to 90 per cent of the
current maximum permitted expenditure of £5,000 for each
dwelling and £5,800 for each unit resulting from a conversion
of a house of three or more storeys may now be paid, both to
owner-occupiers and to landlords (s. 64). There are no precise
rules like those governing intermediate grants as to the nature
of the works which may be grant-aided, provided that the

amount attributed to repairs does not exceed half the total
(s. 63(2)). But grants are not available for the improvement of
second homes (see below), and the Secretary of State has
directed that applications for the conversion of houses with a
rateable value of more than £175 (£300 in Greater London)
which will result in a *reduction* of the number of dwellings
shall not be approved without his consent (Circular 38/77,
para. 14). He has also advised that local authorities should not
normally approve a second grant for the same house within 30
years if the first grant was for works to the full standards, and
that grants for the conversion of non-residential buildings,
such as barns and oast houses, should only be approved where
the dwelling provided as a result makes a useful addition to the
general housing stock in the area and the applicant is not too
wealthy to make a grant from public funds inappropriate
(ibid., paras. 8-13). Grants may be given for the provision of
extra bedrooms by building extensions or by loft conversions,
but the Department of the Environment has advised local
authorities that grants of this kind should be given a low
priority (Circular 160/74, Appendix B, para. 20).

Eligibility

Owner-occupiers, landlords and tenants under fixed term
tenancies with at least five years to run may apply for improvement grants (s. 57(3)). In the case of owner-occupiers a certificate of owner-occupation covering a period of five years must
be given; this effectively excludes applications for second
homes since the certificate covers only occupation as a main or
principal residence (s. 60(3)). In the case of landlords a
certificate of availability for letting covering a period of five
years and in HAAs seven years must be given (ss. 60(5), 73 and
75(4)). Improvement grants for houses for which a certificate
of owner-occupation is given may only be approved if the
rateable value of the house to be improved or converted is less
than a given figure, currently fixed at £225 (in Greater
London £400) for individual houses and £350 (in Greater
London £600) for conversions (s. 62). No grants may be
approved for buildings erected or dwellings provided by conversion after October 2, 1961 (Circular 160/74, paras. 2-3).

Full and reduced standards

Works to the full standard for the purposes of an improvement grant are such as when completed will ensure:

    (i) that the occupants of the dwelling will have exclu-
sive, but not necessarily self-contained, use of all the
standard amenities;

  (ii) that it will be in good repair in relation to its age,
character and locality;

(iii) that it will meet the "10 point" standard in that it
will:

    (1) be substantially free from damp;
    (2) have adequate natural lighting and ventilation in
each habitable room;
    (3) have adequate and safe provision throughout for
artificial lighting, and have sufficient electrical
socket outlets for the safe and proper functioning
of domestic appliances;
    (4) be provided with adequate drainage facilities;
    (5) be in a stable structural condition;
    (6) have satisfactory internal arrangement;
    (7) have satisfactory facilities for preparing and
cooking food;
    (8) be provided with adequate facilities for heating;
    (9) have proper provision for the storage of fuel
(where necessary) and for the storage of refuse;
  (10) have in the roof space thermal insulation as
prescribed for the purpose of home insulation
grants;

  (iv) that it is likely to provide satisfactory housing
accommodation for a period of 30 years.

As in the case of intermediate grants the prohibition on grant
aid for roof insulation which applied until 1978 except in the
case of elderly and disabled applicants has been superseded by
the general provision under the Home Insulation Scheme 1978
for separate grants for insulation work to meet the newly
prescribed standard for improvement grants (Circular 60/78,
Appendix E) (see below).

This list of items for full standard improvement or conversion covers much the same ground as the requirement of

statutory fitness. The only substantial additions compared with the full standard for intermediate grants are in respect of proper electrical and heating facilities and the storage of refuse and fuel. As in the case of intermediate grants, the local authority may reduce the required standard in any respect if it considers that it is not practicable for the full standard to be met at reasonable expense, provided that the dwelling is likely to have a future life of at least ten years (s. 61(4)-(5)). But standards are very rarely reduced. In the period from 1972 to 1976 reduced standard grants were approved in fewer than 4,000 cases compared with more than 600,000 full standard approvals. In practical terms local authorities are much more likely to use their discretion to *increase* standards. Some authorities insist that schemes for rehabilitation with improvement grants shall bring the dwellings concerned up to what are known as Parker Morris standards for new council houses and flats, for example in respect of minimum floor areas for kitchens and bathrooms. Almost all authorities also require that schemes for the conversion of larger houses shall result in the creation of fully self-contained dwellings. A good case can be made for insisting on high standards of rehabilitation and conversion in all cases, and local authorities are clearly entitled to use their discretion to approve or reject applications for improvement grants to that end.

Applicants have no formal right to object to such a policy even if it results in prescribed works which cost far more than the maximum eligible expenditure for grant aid, *i.e.* £5,000 for separate dwellings and £5,800 per unit for conversions, as set out in Table 5.1. The power of the Department of the Environment to raise these limits in exceptional circumstances (s. 64(3)) is rarely exercised. Nor is there any formal way in which objection may be made to the classification of items as repairs and improvements, even if the cost of the repairs exceeds that of the improvements and must accordingly be disallowed to that extent for grant purposes (s. 63(2)). In such cases representations may be made to councillors or senior officials in an attempt to persuade the grants section to relax its standards on the ground that no rehabilitation at all will otherwise be feasible. Alternatively an application may be made to the local authority for an ordinary or a maturity loan (on which interest only is payable until the property is sold) to cover the applicant's contribution. In cases where a standard amenity is lacking it may also be possible to submit an application for an intermediate grant which the local authority has no option but to approve if the relevant statutory criteria are met (see above). In areas where a policy of municipalisation is being implemented, landlords and owner-occupiers may as a last resort offer to sell their properties to the local authority which may then carry out rehabilitation or conversion to whatever standard it pleases.

4. *Repairs Grants*

Grants for the sole purpose of carrying out essential repairs were introduced for the first time under the Housing Act 1974 (ss. 71-72). It was previously considered inappropriate for the state to make any contribution to the cost of regular maintenance or repair, whether for owner-occupiers or for landlords. Since one of the major problems in many run-down areas is lack of maintenance and repair rather than the absence of basic facilities, this policy made little sense. But repairs grants are still limited to Housing Action Areas and General Improvement Areas, and are intended to be approved only in cases of special need.

Eligibility

An owner-occupier, landlord or tenant under a fixed term tenancy which has at least five years to run may apply for a repairs grant provided that the house in question is in a designated HAA or GIA (ss. 57(3) and 71(3)(a)). Owner-occupiers must give a certificate or owner-occupation covering a period of five years, which effectively excludes applications for second homes; landlords must give a certificate of availability for letting covering a period of five years in GIAs and seven years in HAAs (ss. 60 and 75(4)). The dwelling must have been built, or in the case of converted dwellings converted, before October 2 1961 (s. 56(3) and Circular 160/74, paras. 2-3).

The standard of repair

Before approving an application for a repairs grant the local authority must be satisfied that on completion of the works the dwelling will be in good repair (disregarding internal decoration) in relation to its age, character and locality (s. 71(5)). There is no provision for any reduction in this standard. But local authorities clearly have a good deal of discretion on what should be included in the list of prescribed items, provided that nothing that obviously needs repair is omitted. The normal maximum permitted expenditure is currently fixed at £1,500 per dwelling, on which the relevant percentage of 60 per cent, 75 per cent or 90 per cent will be payable. As with other grants, local authorities may submit individual cases to the Department of the Environment for approval of higher cost limits (s. 72(3)).

Undue hardship

The most important consideration in practical terms is the issue of undue hardship. Before approving a repairs grant the local authority is required to consider whether the applicant would be able to finance the work himself without undue hardship (s. 71(2)). This formulation likewise gives local authorities a good deal of discretion to approve applications even if they are not satisfied that hardship would inevitably be caused. The Department of the Environment has suggested that the same approach should be adopted to hardship for the purpose of repairs grants as for the supplementation of other grants from the 75 per cent to the 90 per cent level in HAAs (Circular 160/74, Appendix B, paras. 4-5) (see above). It is therefore arguable that all repairs grants should be awarded at the 90 per cent level. Whatever their method of assessment, however, it is clear that local authorities have not approached repairs grants with much enthusiasm. In the period from January 1975 to September 1977 only 622 repairs grants were approved in the whole of England and Wales. It is hard to justify this restrictive approach, given the fact that many elderly owner-occupiers in inner city areas are dependent on pensions or supplementary benefit. The Supplementary Benefit Commission does make standard payments to owner-occupiers to cover estimated repair and insurance costs. But these payments would not cover more expensive works of the kind appropriate for a repairs grant. There is a strong case for a more co-ordinated approach between the SBC and local authorities on the mechanisms for assisting such persons to carry out regular maintenance and irregular and more expensive repairs and renewals. Similar problems may be faced by some landlords who are dependent on regular rental income from their properties.

5. *Special Grants*

Special grants are an extension of the concept of intermediate (standard amenity) grants to houses in multiple occupation (HMOs). A separate category of grant is necessary for this purpose since, as will be seen in Chapter 6, the essential characteristic of an HMO is that accommodation and facilities are shared by a number of households; standard amenities could not therefore be provided for the exclusive use of the occupants of a single dwelling as is required for intermediate grants (see above). The provision for special grants under the Housing Act 1974 means that the appropriate percentage grant may now be paid in respect of whatever amenities are installed in a HMO (ss. 69-70). Thus if a bathroom with a WC was provided for general use and wash-basins were installed in each of four bed-sitters, the grant would be payable at the appropriate percentage of the amount allowed under an intermediate grant for four wash-basins and one bath, each with hot and cold water supply, and one WC. There is no provision, however, for any grant aid for works of repair other than that which is essential for the installation of the approved amenities.

The rules on eligibility for special grants are for practical purposes identical to those for intermediate grants (see above). Both absentee and resident landlords may therefore apply. So too may the joint or co-operative owners of a house shared by a number of households or individuals. The usual certificates of future occupation covering five years in the case of joint owner-occupation or rented accommodation other than in HAAs, and seven years in the case of rented accommodation in HAAs must be given. The premises must have been built or converted for use as a dwelling before October 2 1961.

There are no formal requirements on standards, except that a fixed bath or shower must always be provided in a separate bathroom (s. 69(3)). But since local authorities are given an unfettered discretion to approve or reject applications as they think fit, they may insist that applicants carry out other works of repair or improvement which do not fall within the scope of a special grant or any other type of grant. In practice special grants are usually administered in conjunction with the other powers of local authorities to secure an improvement in conditions in HMOs. These are discussed in detail in Chapter 6. It is accordingly almost always better to isolate individual dwellings within an HMO, if that is possible, and to make an application for an intermediate or improvement grant under which such works of repair and improvement may be grant aided.

6. *Home Insulation Grants*

Until 1978 grant aid for insulation carried out to achieve the required standard for intermediate and improvement grants was available only for elderly or disabled applicants (see above). This rule was based on the somewhat doubtful argument that insulation was self-financing in that it would result in lower fuel bills (Circular 160/74, para. 7(i)). The more sensible position that it is in the national interest to give positive encouragement to householders to save fuel by insulating their homes eventually prevailed. Under the Home Insulation Act 1978 the Department of the Environment now has wide powers to introduce schemes for grant aid towards specific types of insulation. The first of these is the Home Insulation Scheme 1978, which offers grant aid to householders in the private sector for loft insulation and pipe lagging at a standard rate of 66 per cent of the cost of approved works up to a maximum of £50. Further schemes for other forms of insulation may be introduced in due course.

The details of the Home Insulation Scheme 1978 are set out in Circular 60/78. The scheme applies only to the insulation of roof spaces immediately above the ceiling of a room used for or available for living accommodation. And it is a condition of the approval of any grant that any water tank or pipes in the roof space must be lagged. Grant aid may be paid towards the cost of both insulation and lagging. But a grant may not be made merely for lagging a tank and water pipes. The prescribed standard is defined scientifically in terms of the effectiveness of the insulation and lagging and is somewhat higher than that which is prescribed under current Building Regulations. In practical terms the minimum thickness of standard insulation material which is likely to be required is 80mm for the ceiling (compared with 50mm under the Building Regulations) and 32mm for pipe and tank lagging. The cost of gaining entry to the roof space may be included in the overall cost, but not the cost of making a permanent door or stairway.

The scheme does *not* extend to householders in premises owned by local authorities, housing associations and other public authorities. Applications in respect of houses in the private sector may be made either by landlords or by tenants. But grants may only be made within the limits of the funds specifically made available for the purpose to each local authority. Thus if too many applications are received, some may have to be placed on a waiting list until funds become available.

It must be remembered that grant aid for insulation under the Home Insulation Scheme is separate from that which may be provided for other works of improvement or repair under the Housing Act 1974. This appears to mean that when an application is made for a home insulation grant in conjunction with an application for an intermediate or an improvement grant and funds for the former are not available, the work of insulation may have to be postponed and carried out *after* the works prescribed for the intermediate or improvement grant have been completed, even though insulation to the standard necessary for home insulation grants forms part of the full standard for intermediate and improvement grants (see above). But it should not be necessary for local authorities to delay approval and payment of intermediate or improvement grants until the insulation has been carried out, since the requirement of insulation to the full standard may be waived at the discretion of the local authority. The need to deal separately with applications for intermediate and improvement grants and for home insulation grants is nonetheless unfortunate. It would clearly be simpler for all concerned if insulation undertaken as part of the prescribed works for an intermediate or improvement grant could be treated in exactly the same way as other prescribed works and grant aid paid at the appropriate percentage accordingly.

7. *Grants for Listed Buildings*

All the grants already covered may be paid in appropriate cases in respect of works in buildings listed as of special historic or architectural interest and used for residential purposes. But it is officially recognised that the expenses of repair and rehabilitation in such buildings may be somewhat higher than in ordinary houses if the special character of the buildings are to be retained. To give owners some additional help the standard maximum expenditure limits for improvement grants, currently set at £5,000 (£5,800 for conversions in houses of more than two storeys), have been raised in respect of listed buildings, according to the grade of listing, to the following figures (S.I. 1977 2066):

Grade I   £6,000 (£6,800 three or more storeys)
Grade II*   £5,600 (£6,400 three or more storeys)
Grade II   £5,300 (£6,100 three or more storeys)

It is doubtful whether such relatively small increases provide any real assistance to owners, given the fact that they must themselves contribute the relevant proportion of the total approved expenditure up to these limits and any excess in full. The actual increase in the grant payable in respect of a Grade II listed building, for instance, is a mere 150. Where these standard increases are clearly inadequate owners may make special application for additional discretionary payments by way of grants or loans. Under the Local Authorities (Historic Buildings) Act 1972 local authorities may contribute to the costs of preserving historic buildings by making special grants or loans, though they may impose a condition that access to the general public shall be given and may require repayment if the property is sold within three years. Under the Historic Buildings and Ancient Monuments Act 1953 the Department

of the Environment may also make grants for the preservation of buildings of outstanding historic or architectural
interest. Payments under these statutes are not restricted to the
type of building which is open for public visiting. They may
also be made to owners of private residential houses, provided
that the exterior of the house is visible from the street or otherwise accessible to the public, as for instance under a Town
Scheme jointly sponsored by a local authority and the Historic
Buildings Commission.

Postscript

A number of provisions relating to grants were included in
the Housing Bill published in March 1979 by the outgoing
Labour Government. Provision was to be made for grants for
tenants with effective security of tenure, whether in council
houses or privately rented houses. There were further provisions
to extend repairs grants for substantial or structural repairs to
old houses outside HAAs and GIAs, to permit works of repair to
be included in special grants for the provision of facilities in
HMOs, and to permit the Department of the Environment to
prescribe different appropriate percentages and maximum
expenditure limits for different areas and different types of
house. It was indicated in consultation papers issued before the
Bill was published that repairs grants might be offered for
pre-1919 houses, but that the standard level for expenditure on
the repairs element for all types of grant would be only £1,500.

Further Reading

Useful literature on the grant system is relatively limited.
Reference should always be made to the current issue of the
standard Department of the Environment leaflet, *Your Guide
to House Renovation Grants*, and to any local authority
pamphlets explaining local policies. Accounts of the practical
operation of the system may be found in *Which?* July 1976 and
Roof July 1978. On the preservation of historic buildings see
Left to Rot (1978), published by Save Britain's Heritage,
3 Park Square West, London NW1.

6 Overcrowding and Multiple Occupation

One of the major housing problems in inner city areas is the subdivision of older terrace houses into letting units of one or two rooms with shared or non-existent facilities for cooking and washing. Even if the houses are in good physical repair, living conditions for the occupants may be reduced to an unacceptable standard simply by overcrowding. More frequently overcrowding and subdivision lead to a rapid decline in standards of maintenance and repair. The general remedies in respect of unfitness and disrepair discussed in previous chapters may clearly be used in such cases. But the special problems created by overcrowding and multiple occupation have led to the development of a wide range of special powers and procedures.

Powers to deal with overcrowding have long been an integral part of public health legislation. Provision for the control and supervision of common lodging-houses in which the dangers from inadequate sanitation and ineffective management were most obvious date back to the middle ages. Power to deal with overcrowding in individual and lodging houses alike was introduced as early as 1866 (see Chapter 2). The drawback to reliance on simple abatement notices in cases where overcrowding is the basic problem is that the "offending" occupants are unlikely to have anywhere else to go. One possible solution lies in the provision of adequate self-contained units of accommodation for all households at a realistic price, including single individuals. If this could be achieved excess occupants in overcrowded houses could be rehoused immediately by local councils. While there are long waiting lists for council accommodation, however, and virtually no public provision at all for single individuals, housing departments are naturally reluctant to give automatic preference to people in overcrowded houses for fear of creating a simple method of queue-jumping. In any event it is now widely recognised that the provision of single rooms and flatlets with shared facilities is essential to meet the needs of young people and students, transient workers and families and others who are not eligible for council accommodation and who cannot afford more spacious accommodation on the open market. The main thrust of recent legislation in this sphere has been the development of procedures through which facilities and standards of management in multi-occupied houses may be improved rather than on the elimination of this type of accommodation.

As in other spheres this legislation has been built up in a piecemeal manner with the result that there is a considerable degree of overlap and some inconsistency in the application of the various powers and procedures. In this chapter the measures designed to deal with overcrowding in all types of accommodation will be dealt with first. Those which are primarily directed at the improvement of facilities and physical conditions generally will then be set out and compared with the procedures already described in Chapters 4 and 5. Finally the measures which are primarily directed at the improvement of standards of management will be briefly outlined.

1. *What is a "House in Multiple Occupation" (HMO)?*

Before describing these various procedures it is important to isolate what does and what does not qualify for special treatment as a "house in multiple occupation" (HMO). The statutory definition for most purposes, currently set out in the Housing Act 1969, refers to "a house which is occupied by persons who do not form a single household" (s. 58). In clarifying what this means it is simplest to start from what is obviously *not* an HMO, namely a separate house or flat occupied exclusively by a single family. Because of the difficulty in defining what relatives and other persons could properly be regarded as belonging to a single family, however, an earlier definition based upon the concept of a family had to be abandoned. A household for the purposes of the current definition is best explained, in the absence of further statutory clarification, as a group of people who live and eat communally, whether they are related or not (see generally Circular 67/69). For example if a group of students or two separated wives with their children decided to pool their resources and live communally they would generally be regarded as forming a single household. But where a number of individuals or families, whether related or not, apportion the rooms of a house among themselves for exclusive occupation and share only cooking and washing facilities (as opposed to taking their meals together on a regular basis), it is unlikely that they could properly be regarded as a single household. It has been decided by the courts that it must always be a question of degree whether a group of people constitute a single household, and that a women's refuge in Chiswick with a large and fluctuating population could not reasonably be regarded as a single household even if they did live and cater for themselves on a communal basis (*Simmons* v. *Pizzey* (1977)).

For some purposes it is also necessary to ask whether separate households occupy separate dwellings within the house as a whole. If all of them do, as in a block of flats or a house converted into entirely self-contained units, then the house must be treated for some purposes as a group of separate dwellings rather than an HMO. If some do not, then the house as a whole remains an HMO, but any separate dwelling within it is excluded for the purposes of grants and compulsory improvement notices under the Housing Act 1974. This follows from a statutory amendment introduced as a result of dissatisfaction at a court decision to the effect that a separate and entirely self-contained basement in a house whose upper storeys clearly constituted an HMO formed part of the HMO and could thus be dealt with under the special HMO procedures described below (*Okereke* v. *Brent London Borough Council* (1967). The definition of an HMO under the Housing Act 1974, as opposed to the Housing Acts 1961, 1964 and 1969, is thus "a house which is occupied by persons who do not form a single household, excluding any part thereof which is occupied as a separate dwelling by persons who do form a single household" (s. 129). This means in practice that more generous improvement grants under the Housing Act 1974 are available for such separate dwellings within an HMO. It should be remembered in this context that a separate dwelling need not be self-contained, provided that all cooking, washing and sanitary facilities are for the exclusive use of a single household (see Chapter 5). The facilities for each separate dwelling may thus be on different floors from the principal living rooms, or may be grouped together in a "return," provided that there is no sharing between households.

Thus in so far as an ordinary house is concerned the decision whether or not it constitutes an HMO for the purposes of the Housing Acts 1957, 1961, 1964 and 1969 depends only on the social living arrangements of the occupants. For the purposes of the Housing Act 1974 it depends both on those arrangements and on the physical layout and allocation of rooms and facilities. For practical purposes, however, since the use of the various procedures is generally left to the discretion of the local authority, the classification of individual houses is determined largely by local policy considerations. Disputes on the correct classification of a particular house or part of a house are likely to be productive only in respect of the amount of any grant which may be payable for the installation of facilities and other improvements.

Further complexity is introduced by the special provisions governing tenements and common lodging-houses. All tenements and tenement blocks, which are defined as buildings constructed to provide two or more flats, are regarded as HMOs for the purpose of management orders (see below) Housing Act 1964, s. 69. A tenement or tenement block for this purpose is defined as a building or a part of a building constructed and used as two or more flats. Until 1974 there were also separate provisions for the installation of facilities in tenements and tenement blocks (ibid., ss. 20-21), but they were repealed by the Housing Act 1974. The purpose of these extensions is to permit local authorities to control standards in buildings which might not otherwise be regarded as houses. Common lodging-houses are more restrictively defined as houses "provided for the purpose of accommodating by night poor persons, not being members of the same family ... (in) one common room for the purpose of sleeping or eating ... " (Public Health Act 1936, s. 235). The statutory provisions under the Public Health Acts are mainly concerned with standards of management, though as will be seen that may include compliance with regulations requiring the provision of adequate facilities. But it is clear that common lodging-houses are also HMOs, and may thus be subject to the more general provisions of the Housing Acts.

2. Overcrowding

There are a number of separate procedures for dealing with overcrowding in different types of accommodation.

Overcrowding in dwellinghouses

First in respect of *all* dwellings each local authority has a positive duty under the Housing Act 1957 to prevent certain specific types of overcrowding, covering in broad terms the following (s. 77) (see Appendix I):

  (i) dwellings in which more than two persons over 10 years of age of opposite sexes have to sleep in the same room;

 (ii) dwellings in which there are more than two persons per room (or for two rooms three persons, and for three rooms five persons), or more than a given number of persons per square foot of relevant accommodation, whichever is the less.

Where overcrowding in terms of these standards is established, the local authority may prosecute the occupier (who may be an owner-occupier) or the landlord of a rented house for permitting it, which is defined as the failure to take reasonable steps to secure an abatement after notice has been given (s. 78). Alternatively, in the case of a rented house, it may serve a notice on the occupier requiring abatement in 14 days (s. 85); and if the house is still overcrowded within three months, the local authority may itself apply to the county court for an order to vacate the premises (s. 85(2)). In such cases the local authority would now be under a general duty to provide suitable alternative accommodation under the terms of the Housing (Homeless Persons) Act 1977. There are special provisions in respect of overcrowding caused by children passing the age of ten years designed to give the occupier a defense against any criminal proceedings if he has requested the local authority to provide alternative accommodation (s. 78(3)). Every local authority has a formal statutory duty to inspect premises in its area with a view to preventing over- crowding (s. 76) and to enforce the terms of the statute (s. 85 (1)). Individual households or families may themselves set the procedures in motion by drawing attention to their (involun- tary) breach of the law with a view to getting more rapid rehousing than might otherwise be offered, and if the local authority fails to act, they may with the consent of the Attorney-General, institute proceedings against the local authority (s. 85(4)). But it should be noted that the local authority is authorised to permit *temporary* overcrowding (s. 80).

Overcrowding in HMOs

The provisions for the control of overcrowding in HMOs and lodging houses are somewhat different. Overcrowding is defined as the accommodation of an excessive number of persons having regard to the number of rooms available (Housing Act 1957, s. 90). Local authorities may set their own standards for this purpose by drawing up guidelines for the control of all HMOs in their area and may then serve what is termed a numbers direction on the person in control of any particular house (Housing Act 1961, s. 19). There is a good deal of uniformity in the guidelines which are promulgated for this purpose, since many local authorities have adopted the model prepared by the Department of the Environment. These suggest that a maximum of two persons per habitable room, that is excluding kitchens and bathrooms, should be per- mitted. The service of a numbers direction, however, does not have any immediate effect in so far as those who are currently in the HMO are concerned. It means only that anyone who permits any additional persons to take up residence in excess of the prescribed limit is liable to prosecution (ibid., s. 19(10)). To assist in the enforcement of this the local authority may at any time require the person in control of an HMO to submit a statement of the number of persons currently in occupation (ibid., s. 19(9)).

The practical efficacy of these provisions is largely dependent on the policy of individual local authorities. If the council is prepared to rehouse excess occupants and to punish landlords by criminal prosecution whenever overcrowding is reported, a good deal may be achieved. The difficulty is that in some areas, overcrowding is regarded both by the local authority and by some landlords as a possible means of securing immediate local authority housing for new arrivals. In addition there is usually a serious problem in monitoring and proving the precise number of persons living in an HMO, especially where the number fluctuates from day to day or week to week, or where established residents provide occasional or regular accommodation for their friends and relatives as is often expected within immigrant communities. As a result, the enforcement of numbers directions is often sporadic and ineffective. Nor is there any direct method by which a local authority can be forced either to issue or to enforce a direction, as opposed to a breach of the absolute standard of overcrowding under the Housing Act 1957 (see above). Those living in overcrowded HMOs must accordingly rely on whatever rights they may have under the Housing (Homeless Persons) Act 1977 (see Andrew Arden, *Housing: Security and Rent Control*, ch.10).

3. *The Provision of Facilities*

The purpose of the special procedures under Part II of the Housing Act 1961 is to permit local authorities to require those in control of HMOs to provide basic facilities for cooking, washing and sanitation and to take necessary precautions against fire. The standards which may be required are flexible. Each local authority may prescribe its own set of regulations and guidelines in terms of the number of persons per bathroom or WC or kitchen, and is intended to apply these in conjunction with appropriate numbers directions in respect of the maximum number of persons to be accommodated in the HMO as a whole. The procedures differ from those under the Housing Act 1974 in respect of separate dwellings in that the facilities may be required for joint use by several households or individuals and in that any necessary repairs must usually be separately prescribed under the general provisions of the Housing Act 1957. There are also substantial differences in relation to the amount of grant aid which may be given.

The formal basis for local authority intervention is similar to that of unfitness, namely that the HMO is so far defective in respect of (i) lighting, (ii) ventilation, (iii) water supply, (iv) washing facilities, (v) sanitation, (vi) cooking facilities and (vii) heating facilities that it is unsuitable for occupation by the number of individuals or households in the HMO (s. 15(1)). In practice, most local authorities which use the special HMO powers regularly have prepared a set of guidelines laying down the facilities which they expect landlords to provide in respect of given numbers of persons or households: for instance, a standard form widely used in the London area provides that a bathroom and WC must be provided for every five persons and a wash-basin and cooking unit for each room or household. Where an HMO in which these standards are not met is reported or identified, the local authority may then serve a notice on the person in control, or the person who receives the rent, specifying the works which are required to make the accommodation suitable for occupation for a given number of persons (s. 15(1) as amended by the Housing Act 1964, s. 67). This enables the local authority to prescribe facilities suitable for the number of persons prescribed under a numbers direction. The notice must specify a reasonable time for the completion of the works which may not be less than 21 days (s. 15(3)).

Similar provisions are made for the service of notices prescribing works which in the opinion of the local authority are necessary to provide a means of escape from fire (s. 16). But since the local authority is required to consult with the fire authority before issuing such a notice (s. 16(2)), the requirements are in practice laid down by the officers of the fire authority. In most cases, the fire officer will require the installation of fire doors and of a second staircase for upper storey units. It should be noted that these are not absolute requirements and that the local authority, or the court on appeal, may vary them if they would impose an unreasonable burden in all the circumstances.

Enforcement

The procedures for enforcement are identical for notice served under sections 15 and 16. In the first place, the person on whom the notice is served has a right to appeal within 21 days to the county court, on the ground that the works prescribed are unnecessary or excessive, that the time allowed is insufficient, that some other person is primarily responsible or that there is some formal defect in the notice (s. 17). The court may quash the notice on any of these grounds, though it may decide to ignore immaterial procedural or formal defects (s. 17(2)); in practice it may also confirm the notice subject to any amendment which it considers reasonable in all the circumstances. If the person on whom the notice is served fails to comply within the time specified by the local authority or the court on an appeal, the local authority may either carry out the works itself and collect the cost from the person responsible (s. 18), or else institute criminal proceedings on the ground that there has been a wilful failure to comply (Housing Act 1964, s. 65). The penalty for a first offence is a fine of up to £100 (£500 in respect of fire precautions); for a subsequent offence a term of up to three months imprisonment may be imposed. In many areas, local authorities prefer to use the threat of criminal proceedings to secure action by landlords rather than rely on their powers of default action.

Where local authorities are prepared to devote the necessary resources to enforcement, these procedures should be reasonably effective in securing the provision of basic facilities in HMOs. But there are a number of defects in the law which may cause problems. In the first place, there is no express provision for requiring landlords to carry out necessary repairs in association with the provision of facilities. This means that local authorities may have to serve additional notices under section 9(1A) of the Housing Act 1957 (see Chapter 4) to ensure that such works are included in a rehabilitation scheme. Though similar time periods for completion may be prescribed, different formal procedures for appeal and enforcement must be followed, with the result that delaying tactics by landlords may be pursued with additional ease and effect. In the second place, the provision for special grants is strictly limited to the prescribed cost of the scheduled facilities, so that no assistance may be given to landlords in respect of fire precautions or in respect of repairs unless special hardship can be established for the purposes of a repairs grant (see Chapter 5). This means in effect that grant aid is provided at a lower level for premises in which conditions are often worse than in houses for which full improvement grants are available. This may sometimes be surmounted by identifying separate dwellings within HMOs in respect of which full grants may be paid. But that is likely to result in the prescription of much higher standards, which may in turn put the resulting accommodation out of economic reach for the existing occupants and make landlords even less ready to co-operate. Finally, there is no direct method by which the residents of HMOs may force local authorities to use their powers to insist on the provision of facilities. In some cases it may be possible to establish that the lack of facilities makes the house statutorily unfit, so that local authority must either take some action to make it fit or else rehouse the occupants (see Chapter 4). It would be more satisfactory if tenants in HMOs were given similar rights to those in separate dwellings to make a formal application for the service of compulsory improvement notices.

4. *Management and Control Orders*

Where conditions in an HMO are unsatisfactory primarily as a result of poor management and supervision rather than the absence of facilities the local authority may invoke a different set of procedures. In the first place it may impose a management order under the Housing Act 1961. The effect of this is to subject the landlord to a statutory code of management which the local authority may enforce either by criminal proceedings or by specific orders similar to those for the provision of facilities. If that does not prove satisfactory, the local authority may then impose a control order under the Housing Act 1964, the effect of which is that the local authority itself takes over control of the HMO either with a view to carrying out a scheme of improvement and then handing control back to the owner or else with a view to eventual compulsory purchase. The procedures involved, particularly in respect of control orders, are complex and detailed and will accordingly be described here in outline only.

Management orders

The formal ground for imposing a management order under the Housing Act 1961 is that the HMO in question is in an unsatisfactory state in consequence of a failure to maintain proper standards of management (s. 12(1)). Where a local authority decides to make an order, it must serve a notice of its intention to do so on the owner of the house and also display a copy in a prominent place in the HMO (s. 12(2) as amended). Any person affected may then make representations to the local authority. After at least 21 days the local authority may then proceed to make a formal order subjecting the HMO to the statutory regulations. Further copies must be served on the owner and posted in the house within seven days, but the order comes into effect immediately (s. 12(3)). The owner may appeal against the order on the ground that it is unnecessary (s. 12(4)).

The regulations which are thus brought into force are the Housing (Management of Houses in Multiple Occupation) Regulations 1962 (S.I. 668, 1962). These impose on the person managing the house, who may not be the owner, a series of obligations: all jointly used rooms, stairways, yards and outbuildings must be kept clean and in good order and repair; supplies of water, gas and electricity must be maintained; the proper storage and disposal of refuse and the general safety of residents must be ensured; rooms let after the order comes into effect must be clean and in reasonable structural repair at the start of the letting, and rooms must be put in reasonable structural repair, though the manager is not necessarily responsible for minor items like the replacement of light bulbs and the repair of fixtures broken by tenants; and finally a copy of the regulations and the name and address of the manager must be prominently displayed on the premises. The occupants of the HMO must not hinder the manager by refusing access to individual rooms or failing to give necessary information, must comply with any reasonable arrangements made for dealing with refuse, and must take reasonable care not to cause damage to common facilities. Any person, including a tenant, who knowingly or without reasonable excuse contravenes the regulations is liable on conviction in a magistrates' court to a fine of up to £20 and on a second conviction to imprisonment for up to three months (s. 13(4)).

While a management order remains in force, the local authority may also require the manager of an HMO to carry out works necessary to secure compliance with the regulations (s. 14). These may include works necessary to make good matters neglected before the order was imposed (for instance, any items necessary to bring a room up to the required standard of structural repair) as well as those necessary to continuing compliance (for instance, the replacement of defective basins or cookers in Jointly used rooms or the clearance of accumulated rubbish). The procedure for this purpose is the same as that for notices under sections 15 and 16. Thus the manager may within 21 days appeal to a magistrates court, for instance on the ground that the works are unnecessary or excessive or that someone else is responsible (s. 14(5)), and the local authority may enforce either by doing the work themselves and collecting the cost (s. 18) or by criminal proceedings (Housing Act 1964, s. 65). There is clearly some potential overlap between notices under section 14 in respect of HMOs subject to a management order and notices under sections 15 and 16 (see above). The advantage of the section 14 procedure is that works of repair, either to common parts or to rented rooms, may more readily be included, thus avoiding the need to serve separate notices under the Housing Act 1957.

Control orders

Despite the wide scope and flexibility of management orders the problems involved in continuous supervision and in serving frequent notices on delinquent managers and landlords soon led to the introduction of more far-reaching powers of control. The initial intention under the Housing Act 1964 was to permit local authorities to take direct control of an HMO for a period of up to five years during which it could itself carry out any necessary physical improvements. The general ground for imposing a control order is that living conditions in an HMO in respect of which a numbers direction, management order or notice under sections 14 or 15 has been or might be issued are such that a control order is necessary to protect the safety, health or welfare of persons living in it (s. 73(1)). No advance notice is necessary, but copies of the order must be served on the owners and managers of the house and must be posted in it (s. 73(3)). Any person prejudiced by the order may appeal against it on the ground that it is unnecessary, that a part of the house occupied by the owner could have been excluded, or that there is some formal defect in the order (s. 82). During the time when the order is in force, the local authority has full power to manage the premises, and to collect rents and grant new tenancies (s. 74), though it must make a payment to the owner of one half the rateable value of the property per year. It must also prepare a detailed improvement scheme, setting out the works which the local authority considers necessary to make the premises suitable for multiple occupation and giving details of the financial implications of local authority management (s. 79). Copies of this scheme must be served on the owner, who is given a formal right of appeal against the scheme on the ground that the works are unnecessary or excessive or that the finances of the operation have been improperly calculated (s. 83). If there is no appeal, or if the scheme is upheld with or without amendment on appeal, the local authority must then proceed to carry out the works. The capital cost is then paid out of any revenue surplus retained by the local authority after deducting the quarterly payments due to the owner and any balance outstanding will be entered as a charge on the property (s. 80). When the scheme is complete or at the end of the five year period, the control of the HMO must be handed back to the owner and any revenue balance, less capital expenditure, must be handed back to the owner (s. 86).

The complexity of these procedures was sufficient to deter most local authorities from making use of the new powers. In addition there was a general feeling within those local authorities most directly concerned that it was preferable for the local authority to take permanent control of HMOs whose owners or managers had shown themselves to be incapable or unwilling to maintain reasonable standards. Further amendments were accordingly introduced under the Housing Act 1969 to permit local authorities to proceed immediately from the imposition of a control order to an application for compulsory purchase of the property instead of having to prepare an improvement scheme (s. 63). This means, in effect, that the imposition of a control order may now be regarded simply as an interim step in the process of compulsory purchase of badly managed HMOs which avoids the abuses which frequently occur or continue during the period between the initiation of compulsory purchase procedures and the final approval of the CPO by the Department of the Environment (see below Chapter 8). A few local authorities are now making use of control orders in this way on a regular basis, though in most such cases owners are prepared to negotiate a voluntary sale once the procedures have been initiated.

Common lodging houses

The provisions for the supervision of common lodging-houses are more antiquated and less well developed. A common lodging-house for this purpose is defined in the Public Health Act 1936 as "a house (other than a public assistance institution) provided for the purpose of accommodating by night poor persons, not being members of the same family, who resort thereto and are allowed to occupy one common room for the purpose of sleeping or eating, and includes, where only part of a house is so used, the part so used" (s. 235). This is generally taken to include *only* places where eating or sleeping accommodation is shared, and thus probably excludes rooming houses in which single rooms are let out by the night but no meals are provided. All common lodging-houses within this definition must be registered with the local authority, which may refuse to grant registration if it considers that the premises are unsuitable or that the applicant is not a fit person to act as keeper (s. 238). Unsuccessful applicants have a right of appeal against a refusal of registration (s. 239). Local authorities may also, with the approval of the Department of Health and Social Services, adopt byelaws for the regulation of common lodging-houses (s. 240). A set of model byelaws was prepared for this purpose in 1938, governing all aspects of cleansing, sanitation and maintenance of common lodging-houses, and providing a simple formula in terms of the number of square feet per person to regulate maximum permitted numbers in any given premises. Any breach of these byelaws, where they have been adopted, may be dealt with by way of criminal proceedings in the magistrates court. In addition, individuals may, with the consent of the Attorney-General, institute proceedings in cases where a local authority has neglected to enforce its powers in respect of common lodging houses (s. 298). These special provisions may in certain circumstances prove useful in dealing with abuses in rooming and lodging houses. But the more general provisions of the Public Health and Housing Acts, particularly in respect of statutory nuisances and HMOs, also apply to the common lodging houses and will usually prove more satisfactory.

Further Reading

The most direct and accessible accounts of the law relating to HMOs and common lodging-houses are those prepared by Philag's Public Health Advisory Service: *Practice Notes No. 8 — Houses in Multiple Occupation* (January 1978) and *Practice Notes No. 10 — Common Lodging Houses* (1976): for a discussion of the current administration of the law on HMOs see T. Hadden, *Compulsory Repair and Improvement* (1978), ch. 5 and appendices.

7 Area Improvement

During the 1960s it became apparent in many areas that provision for the rehabilitation of individual houses, whether by financial inducement or compulsory notices, was proving ineffective and that more concerted action would be required if lasting results were to be achieved. The advantages of an area approach are partly administrative. As with schemes for slum clearance and redevelopment it is easier and in theory more economical for local authorities to carry out a rehabilitation programme in a well defined area of poor housing conditions than to deal with individual properties here and there. A more important consideration, however, is what might be termed the dynamics of urban renewal. The objective of area improvement, as opposed to the rehabilitation of isolated houses, is to halt the process of decay in selected areas and to help set them on the path of natural self-regeneration. This is best explained by contrasting the cumulative effects of urban decay and revival.

When an area begins to decline there are a number of forces which tend to accelerate the trend. In the first place a generally low standard of decoration, repair and amenity is likely to discourage owners who set higher standards and may induce them to move elsewhere. It may also become uneconomic for owner-occupiers to spend money on rehabilitation, since the resulting increase in the value of their property may well be a good deal less than the cost of the renovations. Building societies and banks are likely to be correspondingly reluctant to provide finance for purchase or rehabilitation in such areas, since if the borrower is forced to move he may not be able to repay the full amount of the loan. The standard provisions for grant aid are also likely to become increasingly ineffective. From the point of view of private owners, whether owner-occupiers or landlords, there is little incentive to make an application, since the local authority may well insist on improvement to a standard which will involve a very substantial contribution from the owner. Local authorities are in any event reluctant to approve applications from areas which may have to be pulled down, and are discouraged from doing so by the statutory guideline to the effect that the property in question should have an expected future life of 10 or 15 years. As conditions deteriorate, the general expectation that the whole area will eventually be designated for clearance and redevelopment operates as a further disincentive to owners from carrying out any but essential repairs.

Most of these problems are likely to disappear if confidence in the long-term future of the area can be re-established. As individual houses in the area begin to be upgraded, house prices generally are likely to rise and loans for purchase and rehabilitation are likely to become more readily available. New purchasers will be required by building societies to renovate their houses, and the resulting improvement in standards will in time encourage existing residents either to sell as prices rise or else to spend more on their own houses, if only to keep up with the Joneses. The only drawback to regeneration through purely market forces of this kind is that lower-income households are likely to be squeezed out. Established tenants may even be offered substantial cash payments by developers in exchange for giving up protected tenancies, as for instance in such areas of London as Islington. One of the objectives of central government in encouraging area rehabilitation programmes in general and the declaration of HAAs in particular has been to foster the natural processes of self-regeneration without setting in motion this kind of population change, now generally known as "gentrification." Otherwise the existing residents may simply drift into other areas of lower cost and lower quality housing and initiate the processes of decay and decline all over again.

The first legislative attempt to harness these socio-economic forces was the provision under the Housing Act 1961 for the declaration of *Improvement* Areas. More extensive provisions were then made under the Housing Act 1969 for the declaration of *General Improvement Areas* (GIAs). The main purpose was to permit local authorities to give some formal indication in planning terms of their commitment to rehabilitation rather than to clearance and redevelopment. This meant in practice that owners could expect to have applications for discretionary grants approved as a matter of course. In addition local authorities were themselves intended to assist in the process of regeneration by spending money on general environmental improvements such as the provision of new street furniture or tree planting. But there was no direct financial incentive either for private owners or for local authorities. Few areas were declared and the impact in those that were was disappointing.

The first move to increase the financial incentive for improvement was the provision under the Housing Act 1971 for 75 per cent grants to private owners and increased central government subvention to local authorities in certain parts of the country known as Assisted Areas. Then under the Housing Act 1974 higher levels of grant aid were provided for GIAs throughout the country. Local authorities were also given increased powers to insist on the installation of basic amenities through the service of compulsory improvement notices (see Chapter 4). Reasonable results have been achieved by these policies in some better quality GIAs. But on average only about one third of the improvable houses in GIAs were actually improved in the period between 1969 and 1976. And results in areas where the processes of decay and declining confidence had already become established were even more disappointing.

The provision for the declaration of Housing Action Areas (HAAs) under the Housing Act 1974 was introduced specifically to deal with areas in which more positive action than a small increase in levels of grant aid was required. The progressive switch in the late 1960s and early 1970s from a strategy of clearance and redevelopment to one of rehabilitation, already described in Chapter 1, meant that many local authorities were under pressure from local residents to alter their plans both in respect of areas already scheduled for clearance and in respect of those likely to be affected in the future. The basic concept of an HAA was that local authorities should concentrate their resources in relatively small areas. Both private owners and landlords would be encouraged to take up grants for rehabilitation at greatly increased levels. The percentage of approved expenditure which could be grant aided was raised to 75 per cent and in cases of hardship to 90 per cent. Where landlords failed to co-operate, the local authority might then compel them to carry out repairs and improvements by the procedures described in

Chapter 4 or alternatively use its powers of compulsory purchase and carry out the work of rehabilitation itself. It might also encourage local housing associations to buy substandard houses for rehabilitation and reletting. To avoid the long delays which had been experienced under the clearance strategy the necessary action in HAAs was to be carried out within a period of five years. Several hundred HAAs have since been declared, though as will be seen some local authorities have found it more difficult than was expected to achieve the objective of rapid rehabilitation.

The Housing Act 1974 also made provision for the declaration of *Priority Neighbourhoods* in areas adjacent to HAAs or GIAs. This was intended to allow local authorities to take certain preventive measures to control the spread of housing stress into areas which might merit treatment as HAAs or GIAs but which could not be dealt with immediately. Few PNs have been declared.

In the sections which follow a more detailed account will be given of the formal legal basis for designating each of these types of area, and of the specific and general powers available to local authorities within them. This is followed by an account of what has happened in practice and of the ways in which local residents may influence the treatment of their own areas.

1. *General Improvement Areas (GIAs)*

The procedure for the designation of GIAs is now governed by Schedule 5 of the Housing Act 1974, in substitution for the earlier procedures under the Housing Act 1969. The first step is the consideration of a report by any qualified person, whether a local authority officer or not, as to the suitability of any predominantly residential area for treatment as a GIA (s. 28(1)). If the local authority decides to proceed and passes a preliminary resolution to that effect, detailed proposals must then be submitted to the Department of the Environment (s. 28(3)). The department then has one month, or such longer period as it requires to consider the proposal, to veto the scheme (s. 28(5)). If it does not intervene, the local authority may confirm the proposals and must then publicise the designation in two local newspapers and take what other steps are necessary to inform the residents of the designated area (s. 28A). There is no formal requirement that the local authority should consult with local residents in advance of designation. Since the passing of the preliminary resolution will normally be published, however, residents have in practice an opportunity to make representations either to the local council or to the Department, for instance that the area should be extended or that designation as an HAA would be more appropriate. The official view of the Department is that GIAs should be declared in areas of fundamentally sound housing which are capable of providing good living conditions for many years to come, in which the community is stable and predominantly composed of owner-occupiers, and in which there is little housing stress (Circular 13/75, para. 18). The local authority must therefore establish that residents are both willing and financially able to pay their share of grant-aided improvement schemes (Circular 14/75, Memorandum C, para. 9). If it is unlikely that the encouragement of voluntary action by owners will prove effective, and that compulsory powers will have to be used in a systematic way the Department is likely to favour the declaration of an HAA. In practice, however, GIAs have been declared in areas with widely differing characteristics.

The main practical effect of the declaration of a GIA is that higher grants, currently at 60 per cent of approved expenditure, become immediately available (see Chapter 5). This increase only applies, however, to applications made after declaration, so that it may be important for owners to delay making an application until then. From the point of view of the local authority there is also a financial advantage, in that 90 per cent of grants paid in respect of properties in GIAs are funded by the central government compared with 75 per cent in non-designated areas. Declaration also gives the local authority power to issue compulsory improvement notices without a prior request from a tenant (see Chapter 4), and to spend money on environmental improvements both on council land and privately-owned land and to acquire land by agreement (Housing Act 1969, s. 32). Expenditure for such purposes up to a maximum £200 per dwelling in the GIA may be paid by central government (s. 37). To take advantage of these central government subsidies some local authorities designated their own council estates as GIAs, but this practice is now effectively barred by the Department of the Environment.

When the procedures for declaration have been completed it is usual for local authorities to distribute a circular to all houses in the area explaining the effect of designation and encouraging applications for grants. In some cases a local office may be established to assist in processing applications. Some more active local authorities offer all-in grants services of the kind described in Chapter 5. In a few areas the local authority may in addition carry out a house-to-house survey to check on conditions and facilities, with a view to serving compulsory improvement and repair notices in appropriate cases. Intensive action of this kind, however, is now more likely to be reserved for HAAs. But local authorities may be prepared or persuaded to take more active measures, including compulsory purchase and renovation by the local authority itself, to deal with isolated houses which are empty, in serious disrepair or in multiple occupation. The standard powers and procedures under the Housing Acts, discussed in other chapters, are available for this purpose in GIAs as elsewhere, though their use remains a matter for the discretion of the local authority. Responsibility for all these various purposes may be centralized in a joint urban renewal team of the kind often established for HAAs (see below) or may be left to the relevant sections within Housing or Environmental Health Departments.

2. *Housing Action Areas (HAAs)*

The procedure for the designation of HAAs under the Housing Act 1974 is similar to that for GIAs, though the criteria for the selection of areas are more clearly defined. The first step is the consideration by the local authority of a report by any qualified person, whether a local authority officer or not, of the physical state and of social conditions in an area which consists primarily of housing (s. 36(1)). If the authority is satisfied that declaration as an HAA is the best means, within a period of five years, of improving the housing accommodation in the area as a whole, of securing the well-being of the people living there and of ensuring the proper and effective management and use of the accommodation, it may proceed to formal declaration (s. 36(2)). But the authority is bound to "have regard to" any guidance issued by the Department of the Environment whether in general terms or in relation to specific areas (s. 36(3)). And the Secretary of State has power to cancel any declaration or to reduce the area covered within a period of one month, or such longer time as he requires, of receiving notice of the local authority's designation (s. 37). There are additional provisions for the subsequent alterations of HAA boundaries and for the conversion of HAAs into GIAs or PNs and vice versa (ss. 38, 40, 53 and Schedule 5).

The purpose of these measures is to give the Department of the Environment effective control over the selection of HAAs. The current guidelines for this purpose recommend that local authorities should pay special attention to the proportion of houses which lack standard amenities or are otherwise unfit, the extent of overcrowding and multiple occupation, the proportion of privately rented accommodation and the number of households likely to have special housing problems, for instance elderly persons, large families, single parent families and low-income groups (Circular 14/75, Memorandum A, para 12); that relatively small areas of about 200-300 houses should be isolated and dealt with independently (para. 15); that declarations should be phased so as to ensure that sufficient resources in finance and manpower are available to secure a significant improvement in each area within the prescribed period of five years (para. 14); and that HAAs should not be declared in council estates or areas in which there is already a substantial degree of local authority ownership (para. 16). Formal reports on all these matters, backed by suitable statistics, must be submitted to the Department along with the notice of initial designation (s. 36(4)). The Department may not, however, require a local authority to make any declarations.

The effects of designation as an HAA are as follows. In the first place grants up to 75 per cent, or in cases of hardship 90 per cent, of approved expenditure become available to all owners (see Chapter 5). As in GIAs 90 per cent of expenditure for this purpose is funded by central government. The local authority is also authorised to assist private owners in carrying out environmental works, such as external painting or tree planting, on their own premises (s. 45). A central government contribution of 50 per cent of expenditure for this purpose up to £50 per house may be made (s. 46). In the second place the local authority is given an extensive power of compulsory or voluntary purchase to achieve the object of designation, namely to secure the improvement or the better management and use of the accommodation in the area, or to ensure the well-being of the people living there (s. 43). The only obvious limitation on this power is that it cannot properly be used to buy up property for clearance and renewal as opposed to rehabilitation. In the third place all owners are required to give the local authority six weeks notice of any proposed sale of any property or of any forthcoming termination of a tenancy (s. 47). This measure is designed to permit the local authority to control the abuses associated with gentrification and to help ensure that *existing* residents benefit from the designation. The local authority has no formal power to prohibit sales, but may use the threat of compulsory purchase to deter owners from attempting to cash in on their HAA status. It may, however, seek to prevent evictions by initiating a compulsory purchase and applying to the county court for the suspension of any order for vacant possession (Housing Act 1964, s. 72 as amended). The local authority may also require landlords to provide standard amenities without a formal request from tenants, and may of course use any other of its general powers under the Public Health and Housing Acts to compel owners to carry out repairs or to improve conditions in HMOs. Designation as an HAA is effective for a period of five years, but may be extended with the special consent of the Department of the Environment (s. 39).

As soon as an HAA is formally declared the local authority must inform residents by advertising in local newspapers and other appropriate methods (s. 36(4)), and has a continuing obligation to keep them informed on progress and developments (s. 41). Regular reports must also be submitted to the Department of the Environment (s. 42). In practice local authorities usually inform local residents by delivering individual circulars and sometimes by visiting and surveying each house. Continuing information and advice is sometimes provided by setting up a local HAA office in or near the area and by circulating periodic progress reports and newsletters. In some areas all owners and occupiers are interviewed or written to with a view to finding out whether they intend to apply for a grant for any necessary improvements or repairs; if there is no satisfactory response, the local authority may then threaten to serve compulsory improvement or repair notices or in the case of rented properties use its powers of compulsory purchase. To assist in monitoring progress some local authorities keep a separate file on each house in the area. To help avoid interdepartmental wrangles many local authorities have adopted the Department of the Environment's suggestion that multi-disciplinary teams be established to administer urban renewals and rehabilitation programmes (Circular 13/75, para. 28). For instance, a team might be made up primarily of officers seconded from Housing and Environmental Health Departments but representatives from Planning and Estates Departments might also be included. Even where this structure has been adopted the actual implementation of various aspects of the programme, for instance the administration of grants, the service of compulsory improvement and repair notices, the conduct of negotiations for compulsory or voluntary purchase and the actual work of rehabilitation in houses acquired by the local authority, is usually left to the individual departments, so that residents may still have to deal independently with two or three local authority officials at once.

3. *Priority Neighbourhoods (PNs)*

Provision was made in the Housing Act 1974 for the declaration of Priority Neighbourhoods as an intermediate step in areas which are adjacent to areas already declared as HAAs or GIAs. In some cases it was envisaged that this would be primarily a protective measure to prevent overspill from an HAA creating new problems in the adjacent area. In others it was envisaged that the local authority might wish to provide some advance protection in areas which it intended to designate as HAAs or GIAs when resources permitted.

The procedure for the selection and declaration of a PN is similar to that already described for HAAs (s. 52). The guidelines provided by the Department of the Environment suggest that essentially the same criteria for the declaration of HAAs should be applied when it is intended in due course to convert the PN to an HAA, and that though a PN may also be declared with the primary objective of assisting in attaining results in an adjacent HAA or GIA some more positive action in the future should normally be envisaged (Circular 14/75, Memorandum B, paras. 7-10). The effect of declaration as a PN is to give to the local authority the same powers as in an HAA in respect of compulsory purchase and notification of proposed sales or evictions (s. 54). There is no provision for the payment of grants at a higher level than would otherwise be payable. The designation of an area as a PN lasts for five years (s. 54(1)(a)). There are additional provisions for conversion of HAAs or GIAs into PNs (s. 53).

Few PNs have yet been declared. This is largely due to the fact that most of the additional powers granted to local authorities in them are already available under the more general provisions of the Housing Acts, notably in respect of compulsory purchase. There is accordingly little incentive for local authorities to undertake the additional work involved in the processes of declaring and administering a PN.

4. *Rehabilitation Orders*

It should also be noted that temporary provisions were made in the Housing Act 1974 for the conversion of areas or parts of areas already designated as clearance areas under Part III of the Housing Act 1957 into what may be termed rehabilitation areas (s. 114 and schedule 10). The legal effect of a rehabilitation order of this kind is to relieve the local authority of its duty to demolish specified unfit houses in the clearance area and to permit them to be rehabilitated either by the local authority itself or by private owners. The ground on which a rehabilitation order may be made is that the buildings in question are capable of being and ought to be improved to the full standard prescribed for intermediate (standard amenity) grants (see Chapter 5). It may cover isolated buildings within the clearance area or the whole area.

The procedure for making a rehabilitation order is similar to that for CPOs (see Chapter 8). First the local authority must prepare and publish a scheme detailing the buildings affected and must inform owners accordingly (schedule 10, paras. 4-5). The scheme must then be submitted to the Department of the

Environment for confirmation, and if any owner objects he is entitled to a hearing at a public local inquiry or before some person appointed for the purpose (para. 6). After consideration of any report the Department may then confirm the order, with or without amendment. It is also provided that individual owners within a clearance area may apply to the local authority for a rehabilitation order to be made in respect of their properties and that if the local authority refuses it must give its reasons in writing to the owners (para. 3(6)). It has been decided in a test case on this provision that the local authority is in effect the sole judge of whether a rehabilitation order should be made and that the reasons given for refusal need only state that in the opinion of the local authority the buildings in question should be replaced (*Elliott* v. *London Borough of Southwark* (1976)).

5. *Progress in HAAs*

Some four hundred HAAs have been declared since the Housing Act 1974 came into force. This is considerably fewer than was originally anticipated. In a few areas large numbers of HAAs were declared relatively quickly, as for instance in Birmingham where 26 had been declared by the end of 1977. In most areas local authorities proceeded more cautiously and declared only one or two HAAs as part of longer term phased programmes.

Even in those HAAs which have been declared difficulties have often been encountered in achieving rapid results in terms of the number of houses actually rehabilitated. Part of the problem was the substantial cut in housing expenditure during 1975 and 1976, just as HAA programmes were getting under way. But it has also proved more difficult than was initially envisaged either to persuade or to compel many owners to cooperate in rehabilitation programmes. In some areas local residents who initially welcomed the declaration of an HAA have become increasingly dispirited. In others there has been substantial movement in population of the kind which it was hoped could be avoided. But in most HAAs some positive results have eventually been achieved.

To understand the merits and drawbacks of intensive area

action of the kind which declaration of an HAA is intended to facilitate, it is important to distinguish between various types of owner. In most HAAs, as in most GIAs, it has proved relatively easy to persuade a minòrity of owner-occupiers to take advantage of the high levels of grant aid. It has usually proved much more difficult and time-consuming to secure effective action in the remaining houses. Some lower-income owners have been deterred from proceeding with grant applications for fear of being required to carry out more substantial works than they consider necessary and to spend more money than they feel they can afford, even taking into account the offer of grants and loans. Landlords have likewise been reluctant to co-operate in approved schemes of rehabilitation since the result is often a *decrease* in levels of occupancy and thus of rental income combined with an *increase* in current loan repayments. In many HAAs local authorities have thus been forced to adopt a strategy either of serving compulsory improvement and repair notices on a systematic basis or else of resorting to compulsory or voluntary purchase of properties with a view to rehabilitation by their own Housing Departments or by registered housing associations. Where compulsory notices have been served, the end result after further substantial delay has typically been a voluntary or compulsory purchase of the property by the local authority or a housing association. Official figures show that in the period from 1975 to 1977 fewer than one in ten of the compulsory repair and improvement notices served in HAAs resulted in the completion of the works prescribed either by private owners or by the local authority in default. Where local authorities have set out to use their powers of compulsory purchase on a systematic basis, the delays have been somewhat less substantial but periods of up to two years regularly elapse before the local authority can gain control and begin the work of rehabilitation. Widespread purchase and rehabilitation by the local authority is also proving to be highly expensive, not least because of the administrative costs and the very high standards which local authority Housing Departments have set for themselves. In many areas local authorities, with central government support, have also co-operated with independent housing associations by encouraging private owners who wish to sell to sell to a housing association. But this process too takes time, and housing associations have often found that their schemes for rehabilitation exceed the costs limits imposed by central government as a condition of grant aid both for purchase and rehabilitation.

A number of conclusions may be drawn from this initial experience of area improvement programmes. Some commentators have argued that too much emphasis has been placed on rehabilitation of existing houses and that in many areas it would make much more sense in both economic and social terms to embark on a programme of gradual renewal, that is the replacement of small numbers of houses in appropriate terraces or units within the existing street pattern as opposed to wholesale clearance and redevelopment (see for instance Chris Paris, "Housing Action Areas" *Roof*, January 1977). Others argue that the main problem is the unrealistically high standards which local authorities set both for grant-aided private works and for their own rehabilitation, and that more could be achieved if grants were more readily approved at a reduced standard (see Chapter 5). In a number of areas satisfactory if not ideal levels of rehabilitation have been achieved by starting from the position that owners should only be asked to undertake works to a standard which they are prepared to pay for on the assumption that full grant aid and a council loan for any balance is to be paid. This approach is in line with the Department of the Environment's view that "for both social and economic reasons, the primary aim must be to rescue as many ... substandard houses as possible — to bring them up to a decent standard of amenity and a sound state of repair"; and that "if this is not tackled with energy many houses that could be saved will fall into irretrievable decay and many families will have to live in deplorable conditions for years to come" (*Housing Policy Review*, Cmnd. 6851 (1977), para. 10.19). But it is not clear that such a policy is best pursued by the designation of small areas of bad housing for concentrated attention over a five year period as opposed to a more general allocation of the available funds to assist owners to improve bad housing conditions wherever they are located.

6. *The Role of Local Residents*

Many of these poliɔy issues are of obvious concern to residents, both owner-occupiers and tenants, in areas which may be designated for clearance or for rehabilitation. There is now increasing scope for them to influence decisions on the future of their areas if they can work together to produce a practical set of proposals.

In the first place, though there is no formal requirement for advance consultation with local residents in the case of HAAs and GIAs initiated by local authorities, the Housing Act 1974 makes explicit provision for declarations to be initiated by unofficial groups (section 36 and Schedule 5). All that is formally required is the preparation of a report by a "qualified person" setting out the grounds on which the area should be considered for designation as an HAA or GIA. It is the view of the Department of the Environment that a qualified person need not be professionally qualified for this purpose (Circular 14/75, Memorandum A, paras. 3-4), but a report is more likely to carry weight with the local authority if it is prepared in a professional manner and follows closely the format of the local authority's own proposal reports, which in their turn muɔ; comply with the Department of the Environment guidelines. In practical terms it is more likely that a local authority will react favourably to a proposal from a residents association for the declaration of a GIA, since the willingness of local residents to co-operate in schemes for grant-aided rehabilitation is a primary criterion for the choice of GIAs and since the contribution of the local authority in terms of manpower is often much less than for an HAA. But if a local housing association is prepared to undertake the work of surveying, purchasing, and rehabilitating rented accommodation, a proposal for the declaration of an HAA may be equally acceptable. A number of "voluntary" HAAs have been declared in this way at the instigation of housing associations, as for instance in Belfast, with a view to taking advantage of higher levels of grant and of the power of the local authority to compulsorily purchase houses for rehabilitation by a housing association.

Residents may also influence the policies of the local

authority in areas which have already been designated as HAAs or GIAs. It is the official policy of the Department of the Environment that consultations with the local residents in HAAs should continue throughout the period of designation (Circular 14/75, Memorandum A, para. 31). One issue on which pressure may usefully be brought on the local authority is the expenditure of the £200 per house in a GIA and £50 per house in an HAA which the central government is enabled to provide (see above). This money is primarily intended to assist in environmental works on property not owned by the local authority, and may thus be used for street decoration schemes of the kind which residents associations could readily organise and carry through. Pressure may also be put on local authorities, both through local councillors and if necessary by letters or deputations to the Department of the Environment, to adopt more realistic attitudes to standards of rehabilitation or to undertake default works when compulsory repair or improvement notices are not complied with by landlords.

Effective action of this kind depends on a degree of organisation and commitment which it is often difficult to sustain in areas of urban decay. With sensible leadership local residents can play an important role both in the initial stages of declaration by committing themselves to carry out improvements and also by maintaining a continuing dialogue with the local authority team as the months and years pass by. It is particularly important for there to be a flexible organisation through which the local authority team may be kept in touch with what residents want and what they do not want. Practical and financial support for a committee of residents and for public meetings and surveys should always be sought from the local authority. In the last resort decisions on policy and on action in individual cases are a matter for the local authority. But there is sufficient provision in the Housing Act 1974 and in the relevant circulars for continuing publicity and consultation to bring a good deal of pressure on secretive or unsympathetic officials.

Further Reading

The official Department of the Environment guidance on the administration of GIAs and HAAs is contained in Circulars 13/75 and 14/75, as supplemented in Circulars 14/76, 38/77 and 63/78. These are essential reading for an understanding of the current constraints on local authorities. Accounts of practice and results in selected HAAs may be found in *Roof* (see especially the issues of January 1977, May 1977 and July 1977) and in T. Hadden, *Compulsory Repair and Improvement*, Appendices A-E, Centre for Socio-Legal Studies, Wolfson College, Oxford, Research Study No. 1 (1978). The first of the official reports on progress in HAAs and GIAs, *General Improvement Areas 1969-1976*, has recently been published (Improvement Research Note 3/77 (1978), and further reports on research in HAAs are in the pipeline.

8 Compulsory Purchase, Rehousing and Compensation

One of the major objectives of programmes for rehabilitation and area improvement as opposed to clearance and redevelopment is to avoid the massive dislocation of inner city residents which was caused by early slum-clearance programmes. But any scheme for rehabilitation or renewal on a large scale is bound to result in some people being displaced from their homes. In some cases satisfactory rehabilitation cannot be carried out while people are living in the house. In other cases individual houses or terraces are so badly constructed or in such disrepair that it is impractical to do anything but demolish and replace them. In both cases the occupants must be rehoused, either temporarily until the work of rehabilitation or renewal is finished and they can return, or else on a permanent basis in other renovated houses in the same area or elsewhere. It is also necessary for some properties to be compulsorily purchased from landlords or even owner-occupiers who refuse to co-operate in general schemes of rehabilitation. In all these cases compensation may be payable, to displaced occupants for the loss of their home and for disturbance, and to owners for the loss of their property. The purpose of this chapter is to outline the powers and duties of local authorities in these respects. Each of these issues involves a complex area of law with intricate interrelationships which cannot readily be dealt with in distinct sections. But it is convenient to begin with an account of local authority powers of compulsory purchase and entry in HAAs and elsewhere, then to describe their powers and duties in respect of temporary "decanting" and permanent rehousing, and finally, to explain the various types of compensation which may be payable.

1. *Powers of Compulsory Purchase*

Local authorities have a wide variety of powers of compulsory purchase under different statutes. In this chapter it is practicable to deal in detail only with those most widely used in urban renewal programmes, namely the general powers of compulsory purchase for housing purposes under Parts II, III and V of the Housing Act of 1957 and the specific power of compulsory purchase in HAAs under the Housing Act 1974 (s. 43), as opposed for instance to powers in respect of planning under Part VI of the Town and Country Planning Act, 1971, roads under the Highways Acts, 1959 and 1971 and of other local government facilities and services under the Local Government Act 1972. The relevant sections of these statutes, however, govern only the purposes for which compulsory purchase may be sought and sometimes the initial procedural steps. The subsequent procedures for all types of compulsory purchase order (CPO) from the initial notice to treat to the provisions for a local public inquiry in cases where objection is raised and for eventual confirmation by the Department of the Environment are prescribed in the Acquisition of Land (Authorisation Procedure) Act 1946 and the Compulsory Purchase Act 1965. The assessment of compensation for owners and occupiers is also governed by general statutes notably the Land Compensation Acts 1961 and 1973, which are analysed separately below.

Grounds for compulsory purchase

The precise grounds on which compulsory purchase for housing purposes may be sought are differently formulated under the various parts of the Housing Acts. Under Part V of the Housing Act 1957 the local authority must establish that compulsory purchase is necessary for the provision of housing accommodation (ss. 92 and 96). This power is widely relied on for urban renewal programmes outside HAAs and also governs the compulsory purchase of HMOs after the imposition of a control order under the Housing Acts 1964 and 1969 (see Chapter 6). It may be used to acquire houses either for rehabilitation or for demolition and rebuilding, since in either case there will be a qualitative gain in housing accommodation.

There is some doubt whether it may properly be used if there will be a significant decrease in accommodation provided. But it has been decided that an HMO in need of repair and improvement can be compulsorily acquired under Part V, though it is likely in such cases that fewer people will be accommodated after renovation (*Andreister* v. *Minister of Housing and Local Government* (1965)). Under the Housing Act, 1974, which is generally relied on within HAAs, the local authority may justify a compulsory purchase on the ground either that it will lead to an improvement or to the better management and use of accommodation or that it will lead to a general increase in the well-being of residents in the area as a whole (s. 43). It is generally accepted that this power may be used to acquire houses for demolition and clearance as well as for rehabilitation, even if the space is used for other than housing purposes, as for instance in providing a play area or a public open space, since that may well improve the general well-being of local residents.

There is rather less flexibility in the powers of compulsory purchase in respect of unfit houses under Part II of the Housing Act 1957, since there is a presumption built into the statutory framework that such houses should be demolished. It has recently been decided that the power under Part II to compulsorily purchase individual unfit houses which cannot be made fit at reasonable expense but may be made suitable for temporary use (s. 17) may not be used to acquire houses which the local authority wishes to rehabilitate on a permanent basis (*Victoria Square Property Co. Ltd.* v. *London Borough of Southwark* (1978)) (see Chapter 4). Nor may a local authority use the alternative power of compulsory purchase in respect of a house on which a compulsory repair notice has been served but whose owner has successfully appealed on the ground that the work cannot be carried out at reasonable expense (s. 12), unless it is prepared to carry out the necessary work itself forthwith. In such cases the local authority may presumably carry out *more* extensive works than were prescribed in the repair notice. But it could not properly demolish and rebuild. These complexities make it unlikely that the strategy of serving compulsory repair notices to be followed up by compulsory purchase notices under Part II, which is currently being pursued

by some local authorities, will provide a satisfactory long term
alternative to the use of the more general powers under Part V.
Similar problems may arise in respect of houses in clearance
areas declared under Part III of the Housing Act 1957. Before
1974, local authorities were in theory bound to secure the
eventual demolition of all unfit houses in such areas. This
could be achieved either by ordering the owner to demolish the
house at his own expense (s. 44) or else by compulsory purchase,
and demolition by the local authority (ss. 43 and 47). But the
power to retain such houses in use on a temporary basis was
often used over lengthy periods (s. 48). Under the Housing Act
1974 this obligation was removed in respect of areas already
declared if the local authority makes a formal decision to
switch from redevelopment to rehabilitation and secures the
approval of the Department of the Environment for the
necessary rehabilitation order (s. 114 and Schedule 10) (see
Chapter 7). But in areas scheduled for clearance and redevelopment under Part III after 1975 the obligation to secure
eventual demolition still applies, presumably on the ground
that the local authority must have considered and rejected the
possibility of an area rehabilitation scheme. This lack of flexibility is a major drawback to the continued use of redevelopment powers under Part III. Many local authorities accordingly
prefer to use their alternative powers to designate areas for
redevelopment under Part VI of the Town and Country
Planning Act 1971, which permits the compulsory purchase of
a whole area without any underlying obligation to demolish all
existing houses.

Contesting a CPO

When a local authority decides to acquire property compulsorily it must rely on one or other of these various alternative
powers depending on the status of the area in question. It may
not rely on more than one power at once. An owner or other
interested party may then contest the compulsory purchase in
one of two ways. He may seek to have the CPO set aside on the
ground that the local authority has selected the wrong power
or is attempting to use a valid power for some improper
purpose or that there has been some procedural irregularity.

Or he may seek to persuade an inspector at a local public inquiry, and through him the Department of the Environment, that the proposed CPO is unnecessary.

The first of these alternatives is founded on the general principle of administrative law that powers must only be used for the specific purpose for which they are granted. The Southwark case, already referred to, in which the local authority attempted to use a power of compulsory purchase which had been granted to ensure the demolition of unfit houses as a means of securing long term rehabilitation, is an example of this principle. A CPO may also be contested on the ground that the local authority or the Department has not given objectors an adequate opportunity to deal with the real issues at stake or has adopted unfair or improper procedures. Actions to set aside a CPO on such grounds, however, must be taken in the High Court and are likely to be expensive. Even if the case is successful, there is nothing to prevent the local authority from starting the process of compulsory purchase under a more appropriate power or without procedural irregularity all over again. Proceedings of this kind may nonetheless be used as an effective delaying tactic in circumstances in which the passage of time may result in a change of policy. The second alternative relies on the discretionary controls exercised by the Department of the Environment under the Acquisition of Land (Authorisation Procedure) Act 1946. The standard procedure for compulsory purchase requires the local authority to serve a notice on the owner, and other legally interested persons (schedule 1, para. 3). If any person wishes to object to the proposed CPO written notice must be sent to the local authority within the prescribed period (para. 3(1)(b)). If there are no objections the proposal may be submitted direct to the regional office of the Department of the Environment for consideration and authorisation. If objections are received the Department must hold a local public inquiry or hearing at which all the parties may raise whatever arguments they please on the merits of the proposals (para. 4(2)). The inquiry is normally conducted by an independent inspector who is appointed by the Department and reports his conclusions direct to the Department. The Department must then decide whether or not to authorise the proposed CPO. In doing so it is not bound to follow the recommendations of the inspector, though it usually does.

These procedures apply both to proposed CPOs in respect of individual houses and to those involving large numbers of houses in areas shceduled for clearance or redevelopment. In respect of individual properties the owner or occupier may wish to argue that the house is not unfit or that he is in a better position to carry out satisfactory rehabilitation than the local authority. In respect of larger areas local residents may wish to argue that some other scheme, for instance the declaration of an HAA, would be more appropriate or economical in all the circumstances. In either case the inspector is more likely to be impressed if the objector focuses his arguments on the precise grounds on which the local authority is seeking to purchase the property, for instance the need to improve living standards by rehabilitation or to demolish and rebuild, and on the ensuing cost to the public purse than on general objections to an extension of public ownership. But evidence as to the number of properties which the local authority has already purchased but not yet rehabilitated or replaced may be raised as a means of showing that authorisation of the proposed CPO is unlikely to result in any rapid improvement in housing conditions. Though it is rare for area CPO proposals to be turned down in their totality, the inspector or the Department has frequently removed individual properties from the proposed list, particularly in areas where the local authority has set out to use its powers of compulsory purchase in HAAs on a systematic and wholesale basis.

Notices to treat and general vesting declarations

Once the proposed CPO has been authorised, the next step, as prescribed in the Compulsory Purchase Act 1965, is for the local authority to serve a notice to treat on the owner and any person with a leasehold interest which must also be purchased (s. 5). All such persons are required to enter into negotiations with the local authority for the sale of their interests. If agreement as to price cannot be reached the matter must be referred to the Lands Tribunal (s. 6). But the legal formalities for the conveyance of title to the local authority can only be completed when all issues in relation to price and the precise nature and extent of the interests to be conveyed have been settled. These further negotiations may take anything from a few months to several years depending on the complexity of the transaction and the owner's reaction to the local authority's initial assessment of price.

In respect of certain area clearance schemes the position may be different. The Town and Country Planning Act 1968 provides that "any Minister or local or other public authority" may instead of issuing separate notices to treat to each owner issue what is termed a general vesting declaration which has the effect of conveying the land affected by the scheme to the local authority on a specified date without the need for a separate conveyance from each owner (s. 30 and Schedule 3). The procedure is as follows. First the authority must serve notice on all owners in the area informing them of its intention to make a general vesting declaration and requiring them to supply details of their interest in the property affected (Schedule 3, para. 2). The local authority may then fix a date for final vesting not earlier than two months after the service of the notice of intention, and must serve a further notice on all owners informing them of that date (para. 4). After the vesting date the local authority may exercise all the powers of a legal owner of the property affected, and may thus proceed to take possession of any house and to evict any occupier who is unwilling to move. This expedited procedure clearly eliminates any substantial delay after the confirmation of the proposed CPO. But its use is normally restricted to large scale CPOs rather than those which affect individual houses.

2. *Powers of Entry*

From the point of view of a local authority which embarks on a CPO in order to secure an immediate improvement in housing conditions these lengthy delays are clearly unsatisfactory. In the period between the initiation of a CPO and its completion all expenditure on maintenance and repair is likely to cease. Unscrupulous landlords may also seek to increase their interim revenue by bringing in additional tenants hoping to secure a right to be rehoused when the CPO is finally enforced;

alternatively they may winkle out their existing tenants, if necessary by offering them cash payments, with a view to obtaining the higher level of compensation which is generally payable for houses with vacant possession. In an attempt to prevent some of these abuses and to permit more rapid rehabilitation a number of procedures have been developed to allow local authorities to take control of properties before the negotiations on price and the transfer of ownership have been completed.

In most cases of compulsory purchase the earliest point at which a local authority may initiate formal proceedings to gain control is the date of the notice to treat, which may be served as soon as the proposed CPO has been formally authorised by the Department of the Environment. Under the Compulsory Purchase Act 1965 a local authority may at any time after the serving of a notice to treat give 14 days notice to the owner and occupier of its intention to take possession (s. 11). When the notice expires the local authority may take possession of the property, institute proceedings to evict any occupier or take over as landlord in respect of occupants, whether former owner-occupiers or tenants, who are permitted to remain.

In cases where an owner agrees to sell voluntarily in advance of a possible CPO the local authority may often gain entry a good deal earlier. Under the Housing Act 1957 a similar 14 day notice of entry may be served on the owner or occupier as soon as an agreement to purchase is entered into, which is generally interpreted to mean the date of exchange of contracts (s. 101). The main problem in such cases is likely to be the time taken to settle the price to be paid, in that the district valuer may refuse to permit purchase at a higher price than would be payable if compulsory purchase powers were used (see below). In cases where the local authority has served a compulsory improvement notice on the owner and the owner has responded by serving a purchase notice on the local authority (see Chapter 4), however, the local authority may gain entry before the price is agreed since under the Housing Act 1974 a purchase notice is deemed to constitute a notice to treat for the purposes of the Compulsory Purchase Act 1965 (s. 101(2)).

It will be clear that these measures do not solve the problem of the gap between the initiation of a CPO and the point when the local authority can take effective control of the property. Only in the case of HMOs in respect of which a management order has been imposed may the local authority, by imposing a control order, take over as soon as the decision to use powers of compulsory purchase is made (see Chapter 6). In other cases the local authority has power under the Housing Act 1964 to intervene in any formal eviction proceedings by asking the county court to suspend any eviction order pending the resolution of the proposed CPO (s. 72). But it cannot prevent the voluntary termination of a tenancy, which may be accompanied by a handsome golden handshake for the tenant, or a substantial increase in the numbers accommodated. It is arguable that greater powers should be granted to permit local authorities to take temporary control of any tenanted property as soon as the initial proposal for a CPO is published, so that the interregnum between initiation and completion may be eliminated as effectively as in the case of control orders in respect of HMOs and of purchase notices initiated by private owners themselves.

It should be noted in this context that local authorities have wide powers under the Housing Act 1957 to gain entry to any house for the purposes of inspecting conditions (s. 159) and under the Housing Act 1961 for the purpose of ascertaining the number of occupants in HMOs (s. 23(6)). The exercise of such powers does not affect owners' rights of control for other purposes.

3. *Temporary and Permanent Rehousing*

From the point of view of most owner-occupiers and tenants the powers and duties of their local authority in respect of rehousing arising out of compulsory purchase and other compulsory powers are of more direct concern than the formalities of purchase and entry. A distinction must be drawn in this context between the powers of local authorities to assist in the process of rehabilitation by providing temporary and permanent facilities for tenants and owner-occupiers who cannot remain in their houses while the work of rehabilitation is carried out (decanting) and their legal duty to rehouse all persons permanently displaced when houses are closed or compulsorily purchased.

There is no legally enforceable obligation requiring local authorities to provide alternative accommodation for persons displaced in the course of voluntary rehabilitation. But most Housing Departments are prepared to co-operate provided that they are not thereby manoeuvered into giving permanent accommodation to people who would not otherwise be granted a council tenancy. It is normal practice accordingly for the Housing Department to enter into a formal contract with owner-occupiers to provide accommodation only for the period of rehabilitation, after which they must return to their own houses. In the case of rented houses it is usual to add a provision to the effect that if the occupants who are rehoused are unwilling to give up their "temporary" council houses or flats and return to their former houses or flats the Housing Department may nominate an alternative tenant. This stipulation has been found to be necessary to avoid the abuse of rehousing facilities by landlords who wish to gain vacant possession, since tenants who are granted council accommodation are often reluctant to give it up, not least because there is likely to be an increase in the rent of their original accommodation after rehabilitation. These practices are given formal statutory recognition under the Housing Act 1974 as "housing arrangements" with a view to facilitating those on whom compulsory improvement notices are served (s. 86). Tenants and landlords may make formal representations at a time-and-place meeting or enter an appeal on the ground that the proposed housing arrangements are unsatisfactory (ss. 85(5), 89(6)(b), 91(2)(g) and 91(3)(b)).

Where the occupants of a house are legally required to move the obligations of the local authority to rehouse them are more precisely defined. Under the Land Compensation Act 1973 (as amended) local authorities must provide "suitable alternative residential accommodation on reasonable terms" to all persons who are permanently displaced as a result of (i) a compulsory purchase order, (ii) a closing, demolition or clearance order or undertaking, (iii) a compulsory improvement notice or undertaking, or (iv) a redevelopment or improvement scheme unless such accommodation is "otherwise available" to them (s.39).

It has been decided that this provision does not automatically entitle eligible households to go to the top of the local waiting list for permanent council housing, and that in some circum-.stances the local authority may fulfil its duty by offering temporary accommodation:

> *R. v. Bristol Corporation ex p. Hendy (1974)*
> The tenant of a basement flat which had been closed as unfit was offered and accepted temporary council accommodation with a promise of an offer of permanent accommodation as soon as was possible. He then sued the council on the ground that it had failed to carry out its statutory duty to provide suitable alternative accommoda- tion on reasonable terms, claiming that he should have been given priority over other households on the waiting list and in addition the same security of tenure as he had enjoyed in his flat. It was held that the council had ful- filled its duty: though the council might well take into account the fact that he had been displaced under a clos- ing order, that did not mean that he took priority over everyone else on the housing list; his circumstances must be considered along with the others on the list and a fair decision made between them (per Lord Denning M.R.)

The fundamental issue is whether the accommodation offered is a suitable alternative in all the circumstances. Those who are displaced may reasonably expect to be offered some choice, in respect both of the type of accommodation and of its location. The precise number of suitable offers which may be turned down before the local authority's duty is exhausted is not specified and probably depends on local practice in such matters. In many areas it is established that if two reasonable offers are rejected by a household it loses its place at the top of the waiting list. This may equally be applied to cases of rehous- ing under the Land Compensation Act.

It should be noted that the duty to rehouse does not apply to trespassers or to licensees who have been permitted to occupy the house pending improvement or demolition (s. 39(3)), nor to persons not residing in the house when the CPO was first published or the relevant order or undertaking was made (s. 39(6)). But this does not affect the more general duty of local authorities to provide housing accommodation under the

Housing (Homeless Persons) Act 1977. The interpretation of that duty is discussed in detail in Andrew Arden, *Housing: Security and Rent Control* (1978) (see ch. 10).

4. Compensation

Owner-occupiers, landlords and tenants who are affected by compulsory purchase orders, clearance, closing or demolition orders, compulsory improvement notices and schemes for redevelopment or improvement may be eligible for two forms of compensation: a payment in respect of the value of any property taken from them and a payment in respect of the fact that they have been required to give up their home and move elsewhere. The first of these dates back to the nineteenth century and is currently governed by the Land Compensation Act 1961. The second is a recent innovation under the Land Compensation Act 1973 and is designed to give some recompense to those who do not own their own homes but have been forced to give them up. Since it is likely to affect a greater number of people the new form of compensation is dealt with first.

Compensation for displacement

The most substantial form of compensation for displacement is the *Home Loss Payment* under the Land Compensation Act 1973 (as amended) (s. 29). This is intended for households who have lived in the same house or flat for a long enough period to entitle them to compensation for the loss of an established home in the widest sense of that word. Only those who have occupied their house or flat as an owner, as a tenant for the purposes of the Rent Acts or as an employee for a period of at least five years before the date of displacement are eligible (s. 29(2)). Trespassers and licensees are thus excluded. As in the case of the duty to rehouse the statute covers all cases in which the household is permanently displaced as a result of (i) a CPO, (ii) a closing, demolition or clearance order or undertaking, (iii) a compulsory improvement notice, or undertaking, or (iv) the acquisition of property by a local authority for the purposes of redevelopment or improvement (s. 29(1)). It extends in addition to households which move in anticipation of a CPO before they are legally required to do so provided that the move is made after the authorisation of the proposed CPO (s. 29(3)), and to tenants who are displaced as a result of a voluntary sale by an owner (s. 39(6)). Local authorities *may* but are not obliged to make the equivalent of a Home Loss Payment to owners who voluntarily sell property in respect of which a CPO might have been made (s. 32(7)). Owners who require the local authority to acquire their property by serving a blight notice (see below) are not eligible (s. 29(5)).

Applications for a Home Loss Payment must be made in writing within six months before or after the date of the displacement (s. 32(1)). The amount of the payment is fixed by statute as *either* £150 *or* three times the rateable value of the house or flat up to a maximum of £1,500 whichever is the larger (s. 30). It is thus a conventional payment rather than an attempt to assess accurately the differential impact on different households, and is made equally to those who want nothing more than to be moved from what they regard as a slum and to those who object strenuously to being forced to move from what they regard as perfectly satisfactory accommodation. Payment must be made within three months of the applications or of the date of displacement, whichever is the later (s. 32(2)).

Provision is also made under the Land Compensation Act 1973 for a further less substantial *Disturbance Payment* in respect of the expenses of moving. This, like a Home Loss Payment, is payable to any household which is permanently displaced as a result of (i) a CPO, (ii) a closing, demolition or clearance order or undertaking, (iii) a compulsory improvement notice or undertaking, and (iv) the acquisition of property by a local authority or housing association for the purposes of redevelopment or improvement (s. 37(1)). But there is no requirement of five years residence or that the household should have a tenancy, provided that it is in lawful occupation of the accommodation (s. 37(2)(a)). Licensees are accordingly eligible, though trespassers are not. Those who are eligible to receive compensation (other than site value) in respect of the compulsory purchase of a legal interest in the property are also excluded, since they should receive a similar payment for disturbance as part of their overall award (see below) (s. 37(2)(b)). Local authorities have a similar discretion as in the case of Home Loss Payments to make a payment to households which are displaced but not technically eligible (s. 37(5)). The amount of a Disturbance Payment is not fixed at a precise sum but is in theory assessed as the "reasonable expenses of the person entitled in removing from the land from which he is displaced" (s. 38(1)(a)). In practice local authorities usually fix a standard sum — a payment of £85 was regularly made — and may give applicants the impression that it is fixed by law. Any household which regards such a standard amount as inadequate to cover its actual expenses in moving may make a specific claim for a larger amount and if agreement is not reached may take the case before the Lands Tribunal (s. 38(4)).

A Disturbance Payment is also payable to businesses which are displaced but have no other compensatable interest in the property affected; in such cases the amount is assessed as the loss which the owner will sustain as a result of having to move (s. 38(1)(b)). Assessment in such cases is a complex matter which cannot be dealt with here.

Compensation for loss of property

The provisions for payment of compensation in respect of loss of property are much more complex than those in respect of displacement and will only be outlined here as they are likely to apply in straightforward cases involving residential property. Where commercial and other types of property are involved competent professional advice should always be obtained.

The twin foundations of the system of compensation for residential properties are first that owners should be paid the current market value of the property taken, and second that unfit houses should be regarded as worthless and that their owners should accordingly receive only the value of their sites. The injustice of this second principle, however, given the increasingly wide application of the concept of unfitness, has led to the introduction of a number of significant exceptions designed to give owner-occupiers the right to receive what amounts to market value for unfit houses.

Fit properties

The provisions for compensation in respect of fit properties are contained in the Land Compensation Act 1961. This sets out six basic rules of assessment, notably that the value of the property taken shall be fixed at the amount which it would realise if offered by a willing seller on the open market (Rule 2), and that no special premium shall be given on account of the fact that the owner is being forced to sell (Rule 1) (s. 5). It is also provided that no account is to be taken of the effect on the market price, whether an increase or decrease, of the proposed development or scheme for which the CPO has been initiated (s. 6). Any depreciation in the value of the property resulting from the anticipated compulsory purchase, on the other hand, must be ignored (s. 9), and account may be taken of any increase in value in respect of any potential development for which planning permission might reasonably have been expected to be granted had there been no proposed local authority intervention (ss. 14-16). The intention of these provisions is to ensure that owners neither reap a benefit nor suffer a loss as a result of local authority intervention, but obtain for their property the best assessment of what it would have been worth had there been no such intervention. Most people regard this as a reasonably fair basis for compensation. But there are many objections, as will be seen, to the way in which the rules are applied in practice in run-down areas of the kind which are typically subject to local authority CPOs.

Unfit properties

In respect of unfit houses the starting point is not market value but cleared site value. This is said to follow from the provisions under the Housing Act 1957 which permit local authorities to require the owners of unfit houses which cannot be made fit at reasonable expense to demolish them and clear the site at their own expense. This formal obligation, however, is seldom enforced and the argument that unfit houses are worthless is not very convincing. In any event it is now recognised that such houses have a real market value and that owner-occupiers at least should be compensated for their compulsory purchase. Under the Housing Act 1957 certain classes of owner-occupier are eligible for what is termed an owner-occupiers supplement which in effect brings the compensation payable to them in respect of unfit houses up to full market value (s. 61 and Schedule 2, Pt. II). This principle has been extended by the Housing Act 1969 so that all owner-occupiers of unfit houses are now entitled to compensation at full market value, provided that they have acquired their house at least two years before the proceedings for compulsory purchase were initiated and had no reason to believe that a CPO was likely to be made (s. 68 and Schedule 5). This means that except in a few rare cases in which the CPO was commenced before 1968 established owner-occupiers of unfit houses are treated in the same way as those of fit houses, and that the cleared site value rule applies only to landlords.

There is a further but less far-reaching provision under the Housing Act 1957 designed to give some additional compensation over cleared site value in respect of unfit houses which have been well-maintained (ss. 30 and 60). A well-maintained payment may be made in respect of any house which though statutorily unfit has been well looked after and is payable either to an owner-occupier or to a landlord or tenant who can show that the maintenance of the house has been carried out at his expense. But since a well-maintained payment cannot be made in any cases where compensation is payable at full market value, its primary application is to landlords or tenants. The amount payable is eight times the rateable valuation of the house, provided that the total of the cleared site value and the well-maintained payment does not exceed market valuation (schedule 2 as amended by S.I. 1972 No. 1792). Applications for a well maintained payment following compulsory purchase or closure under Part II of the Housing Act 1957 must be made within three months of the notice to treat or closing order (s. 30(1)); payments in respect of houses to be cleared or acquired under Part III may only be made on the authorisation of the Department of the Environment and there is no formal provision for any application (s. 60).

Disturbance

Any person who is entitled to receive market value

compensation for the compulsory purchase of his property may in addition include a claim for disturbance. There is no express statutory authorisation for such claims. But it has long been established that expenses or losses unavoidably incurred as a result of a compulsory purchase are recoverable as a separate head of compensation. Where the amount of compensation is expressly limited by statute, as in the case of cleared site value compensation for rented unfit houses, this claim is excluded, though a similar amount will often be payable under the Land Compensation Act, 1973 (see above). The sum which may be claimed for disturbance is not fixed, but must be itemised and justified in each individual case. Residential occupiers may thus claim the expenses incurred in moving themselves and their effects to their new accommodation, and also for the replacement of any items which were suitable in their old house but cannot reasonably be used in the new one, as for instance curtains or carpets.

Business owners may in addition claim for any loss of profit resulting from the move. Those who have a compensatable interest in the premises in which they work, for instance the owners of a shop, may simply add such a claim on a non-statutory basis. Those who have no such compensatable interest must rely on the Land Compensation Act 1973 (s. 37) (see above). The basis of assessment is for practical purposes the same. The amount of the statutory claim is expressly stated to be the loss which will be suffered as a result of the requirement to quit, taking into account the expected future life of the business in its original premises and the availability of other suitable premises (s. 38(1)(b) and (2)). This is simply a reformation of the established rules for non-statutory claims for disturbance in combination with a claim for the market value of the premises.

Assessment and appeals

The compensation payable in all these cases both for the property taken and for disturbance is normally assessed in the first instance by the local authority in the light of its own information or that which the applicant supplies. Local authorities often seek to apply standard figures both for the value of houses of a particular type and for disturbance payments, and sometimes give the impression that these figures are laid down by the local district valuer who exercises a general supervisory jurisdiction over all assessments of compensation. The final authority in all cases, however, is the Lands Tribunal and those eligible for compensation for loss of property or disturbance have a formal right under the Land Compensation Act 1961 to have the amount determined by that body (s. 1). In practice, local authorities are often prepared to make a slightly higher offer to any person who raises serious objections to their initial offer, though this will usually take some time. But where there is a substantial difference between the offer by the local authority and the amount claimed by the displaced person the case must be argued before the Lands Tribunal. There is nothing to prevent anyone from conducting such a case himself, though it is usual to employ a lawyer or professional valuer who has experience of the way in which the proceedings are conducted.

What is market value?

The central issue in most cases involving residential as opposed to business property is likely to be the assessment of market value. Though the Land Compensation Act 1961 requires any diminution of value which has been caused by the scheme in question to be ignored, it is the normal practice of local authorities and district valuers to set a relatively low standard price for typical houses in run-down areas affected by planning blight. The justification for this is the prevalent assumption that even in the absence of local authority intervention property values in such areas would have declined. This may not be justified. It is equally arguable in many areas that the primary cause of the decline in values has been the anticipation of redevelopment. If this can be established, the correct basis for valuation is not the prevailing market price in the area affected by the scheme but the prevailing market price for similar houses in areas in which there has been no planning blight. If such a comparable area can be found, the best evidence to present to the Tribunal is of current house prices there. If no such direct comparison can be found, it may then be necessary to argue that a similar proportional increase in house prices from the date when planning blight began to have effect should be assumed as for other types of property in the region. It should also be noted that there is no statutory basis for the widespread view that the proper date for the valuation is the date of the notice to treat. The correct view, as held in *West Midland Baptist (Trust) Association* v. *Birmingham Corporation* (1970), is that the property should be valued either as at the date on which possession is taken or as at the date on which the final assessment of value, for instance on appeal to the Lands Tribunal, is made. In a period of rapid inflation it may therefore be an advantage to freeholders to have the date of valuation put back as far as possible, since whatever figure is taken to be the notional market value at any earlier date must be adjusted upwards accordingly.

Blight Notices

The provision of compensation at a notional market value on the assumption that there has been no local authority intervention is theoretically justifiable for those who are prepared to remain in their houses until a CPO is enforced. It does not alter the fact that actual market values for property in blighted areas are likely to be much lower, not least because any purchaser of an unfit house with knowledge of the impending scheme is entitled to cleared site value only (see above). The effect is that as soon as the likelihood of compulsory purchase becomes public knowledge owners are effectively barred from selling. To meet this difficulty provision was introduced under the Town and Country Planning Act 1959 to permit owners who could not sell their property at a reasonable price as a direct result of redevelopment or other planning schemes to require the local authority to purchase them. The current provisions are contained in the Town and Country Planning Act 1971, Part IX, as amended by the Land Compensation Act 1973, Part V. These permit any owner of property which is already or is likely to be subject to a CPO to serve what is now called a "blight notice" on the authority by which the property is liable to be acquired, provided that he can establish that he has attempted and failed to sell at a reasonable price on the open market (s. 193). The authority must then purchase the property at the price which it would have to pay by way of compensation following a CPO unless it can show that the property is not covered by the statutory provisions. The most important exemption in this context is that which frees the local authority of any obligation to purchase in cases in which it does not intend to compulsorily purchase the property for any purpose within a period of ten years (s. 194 as amended by the Community Land Act 1975, schedule 10, para. 6).

Further Reading

The topics covered in this chapter are not covered conveniently or comprehensively either in standard practitioners' texts or in simpler summaries of the law. The best and most readily intelligible account of the procedures for compulsory purchase and the rules on compensation will be found in Keith Davies, *Law of Compulsory Purchase and Compensation*, 3rd ed. (1978); a straightforward statement of the grounds on which a compulsory purchase order may be contested in the courts may be found in S. A. de Smith, *Constitutional Law*.

9 Conclusions: Towards an Integrated Code

It will be clear from the preceding chapters that the law governing both voluntary and compulsory rehabilitation is complex and confused. The principal cause for this is the superimposition of a series of different legislative policies, notably the abatement of statutory nuisances under the Public Health Acts, the clearance of unfit houses both individually and in clearance areas under the earlier Housing Acts and the encouragement or compulsion of rehabilitation and improvement under more recent Housing Acts. There are in addition a number of separate codes for dealing with particular types of housing, notably houses in multiple occupation, which must also be fitted in with the general rules and procedures applicable to all housing. The availability of a large number of different powers is in some cases an advantage from the point of view of local authorities, in that technical difficulties encountered under one set of procedures may often be avoided by relying on another. But the complexity and overlapping of the various powers and procedures often causes serious problems in their application and enforcement. The clear legislative intention that all unfit houses must be either closed or improved linked to the increasingly high standard for fitness, for instance, creates serious legal problems for any authority which wishes to pursue a policy of gradual or temporary improvement. The very high standards which are regularly required as a condition of repair and improvement grants create similar economic problems for owner-occupiers and landlords who cannot afford the full cost of rehabilitation to ideal standards. The current procedures for enforcing compulsory repair and improvement, notably compulsory improvement notices, have likewise made it administratively and legally difficult for local authorities to achieve satisfactory levels of compliance.

In suggesting a new and more integrated legal framework through which some at least of these difficulties might be eased it is important to draw a distinction between housing law and housing policy. Political parties at both national and local levels naturally like to be able to promise and to implement new housing policies which are observably different from those of their opponents. It is this tendency which has resulted in much of the current complexity of the law, since new policies are usually enacted without an adequate consideration of their impact on the existing legal framework. If a new legal framework is not to suffer the same fate it is therefore essential to incorporate a good deal of flexibility so that new political and financial policies may be implemented without recreating the legislative chaos which we have inherited from the past. The proposals which follow are accordingly designed to create a coherent and workable set of procedures which may be used in the pursuit of a wide range of different housing policies. This approach will not be palatable to those who seek immediate solutions to social problems by mandatory legislation. But there is enough evidence both of the importance of administrative as opposed to legal structures in achieving social goals and of the inherently lengthy time-spans involved in any housing programme to justify an attempt to improve the basic tools of all housing policies without prescribing exactly how they should be used.

The basis for an integrated code of procedures which should meet most objectives is the isolation of four levels of action:

(i) the maintenance of a reasonable level of repair in existing accommodation;

(ii) the implementation of schemes for major rehabilitation;

(iii) the closing of accommodation which cannot economically be dealt with by the repair or rehabilitation procedures;

(iv) the compulsory purchase of property where it is necessary to achieve any of these objectives.

For each of these a simple set of procedures is required which will enable both local authorities and occupiers, whether in the public or private sector, to initiate appropriate action and to ensure that it is completed. These will be outlined in turn.

The chapter ends with a brief discussion of the possibility of bringing together all aspects of housing law and administration under a single jurisdiction to avoid the existing fragmentation of the various interrelated issues of rent, security of tenure and standards of repair, which must at present be dealt with separately in rent tribunals and rent assessment committees, in county courts and in magistrates courts.

A disrepair procedure

There are currently two different methods by which local authorities may compel owners to repair their houses; the statutory nuisance procedure under the Public Health Acts and the procedure under the Housing Act 1957 in respect of houses in substantial disrepair (see Chapter 4). In addition tenants of both private and public landlords may seek to enforce their landlords' obligations under the statutory repair covenants implied in most weekly or monthly tenancies under the Housing Act 1961 or by themselves initiating proceedings for the abatement of a statutory nuisance under Section 99 of the Public Health Act 1936. None of these procedures formally involves any consideration of the cost of the repairs nor their relation to the rent, though in practice courts are likely to take both factors into account in deciding on what order to make.

There is a strong case for the enactment of a single simplified procedure through which both local authorities and tenants might enforce a single standard of reasonable tenantable repair similar to that prescribed under the Housing Act 1961. A formulation of this kind, which could be linked with the preparation of a model tenancy agreement for local authorities, housing association and other owners, specifying precisely the minimum duties of landlords, would be a considerable advance on the existing but less precise and intelligible concepts of statutory nuisance and substantial disrepair, not least because of the restrictive approach to statutory nuisances in recent court cases. This obligation should be enforceable by any lawful occupier, including licensees, or by a local authority against any owner, though it is highly unlikely that proceedings would be taken against owner-occupiers except in cases in which there was a clear risk of injury or prejudice to someone other than the owner.

In purely procedural terms the best features of repair notices under both the Public Health and the Housing Acts should be drawn on. It should be open to individual tenants and to licensees *either* to seek the assistance of their local authority which might then serve a repair notice on the person responsible *or else* to initiate proceedings in the relevant court without reference to the local authority, as for instance where the local authority itself is the landlord. Where disrepair is established the primary remedy should be a court order directing the person responsible to put matters right. But the court should also be authorised to impose a single or continuing fine on defaulting landlords in appropriate cases. In cases where the local authority has served a repair notice it should be authorised to carry out the works itself in default of action by the person responsible within a reasonable period; the cost might then be collected from the person responsible by proceedings in the relevant court or through a court order attaching a reasonable proportion of the rent otherwise due to the landlord. This would enable local authorities to take action to improve conditions without waiting for a court hearing, which is the main drawback with current proceedings under the Public Health Act in certain areas. Where there is a need for urgent action the local authority should be entitled as at present to serve a special notice requiring immediate action by the person responsible, and if that is not complied with within 24 or 48 hours to carry out the works in default. In any case where the local authority acts in default it would then have to establish that its action was reasonable in any subsequent proceedings to collect the cost from the person responsible. The procedure would thus encourage remedial action by the local authority as the first step of enforcement, leaving liability for the cost to be settled at a later stage. The right of tenants to carry out works themselves and deduct the cost from their rent, provided that they have given reasonable notice to their landlords, should also be given clear statutory backing.

It should not be necessary in normal circumstances to impose any reasonable expense criterion in respect of the relatively minor works required under the proposed repair notice procedure. Where the works required are unreasonable in relation to the level of the rent or the resources of the person responsible, the relevant court should be entitled to order the local authority to make whatever grants or loans may legitimately be made and to enter the amount recoverable from the owner as a charge on the property. This is most likely to be required in cases where the level of rent has been controlled by statute. To avoid abuse by landlords who might seek to have regular repairs carried out for them by the local authority, it might be necessary to establish that an arbitrary proportion of the rent should be spent on repairs, and that where this amount has not been spent over a specified period of years the owner should himself be required to contribute any balance.

A rehabilitation procedure

Any procedure for the compulsory rehabilitation of houses or flats must be more extended than that for relatively minor repairs given the more substantial nature of the work involved. The underlying objective should be to permit local authorities to require owners to carry out schemes of rehabilitation to the same or a similar standard as the local authority would itself carry out if it acquired the property. If this is not possible, the local authority may well be reluctant to enforce a rehabilitation notice. But it is equally necessary to ensure that the provision for grants and loans for such works are sufficient to enable owners to comply without suffering a short or long-term financial loss. It follows that the standard which local authorities may prescribe for grant-aided works and for compulsory rehabilitation should be the same, and that if a local authority prescribes works to a standard which requires an unreasonable contribution from the owner, given current grant levels, it should be required to fund the capital cost of any excess itself.

The procedure for achieving these objectives should be modelled on existing procedures under the Housing Acts in respect of unfit houses and compulsory improvement notices (see Chapter 4) but designed to eliminate unnecessary delays. The first step would be the service on the owner of a notice setting out the works necessary to bring the accommodation up to the local authority's chosen standard. A period of three to four weeks should then be allowed within which the owner might either require the local authority to arrange a meeting with him and his advisers with a view to reaching a compromise undertaking accept'able to both sides or else enter an appeal against the notice to the relevant court. Where the works prescribed for rented accommodation were estimated to exceed a reasonable expenditure limit, in that the landlord's return from the property, after allowing for any grants and loans and any rent increase was less than his current income, the landlord should be permitted to serve a purchase notice on the local authority. The local authority might then either accept the purchase notice and take immediate possession of the property with a view to carrying out the stated works within a prescribed period, or else agree to make an additional contribution to cover any excess costs over the reasonable expenditure limit, or else reduce the standard of the works required. If neither an appeal nor a purchase notice were made, the rehabilitation notice would then become effective and the owner would be required to carry out the prescribed works within the period specified by the local authority. On the expiry of that period the local authority would be required to carry out the works in default and might then collect the owner's contribution, plus an appropriate charge for administration, by court proceedings.

This procedure is designed to ensure that when compulsory rehabilitation notices are initiated the prescribed works must be carried out either by the owner or by the local authority, and thus to deter local authorities from using their powers to induce landlords to sell their properties. But local authorities should be permitted in cases in which they have carried out the prescribed works in default to initiate compulsory purchase proceedings in the usual way. It might also be necessary, given the reluctance of some local authorities to use their compulsory powers, to give occupants of substandard houses the right to make an application to the relevant court for the local authority to show cause why it should not issue a rehabilitation notice. In all cases where rehabilitation could not be effectively carried out while the premises were occupied the local authority should be required to provide suitable alternative temporary accommodation, but should be permitted to nominate tenants for the newly rehabilitated premises if those who have been rehoused are unwilling to return. Any other

tenancy which the landlord attempted to create in the mean-
time should be statutorily void and the landlord should be
required to compensate any person who suffered loss or inconvenience as a result.

A closing procedure

The principal problems in relation to current closing
procedures are the complex interrelationship of closing orders,
rehousing and the procedures for requiring owners of unfit
houses to make them fit, and the fact that standards of fitness
are set so high that it is impractical for local authorities to
enforce the law. What is required to surmount these difficulties is a realistic definition of houses which must be immediately closed and a simple procedure for enforcement. The fact
that as many as 5 per cent of the total housing stock in England
and Wales was reckoned to be unfit in 1976, as shown in
Chapter 1, is an indication of how far the current conception
of fitness has strayed from the original statutory intention that
no-one should be permitted to continue to live in an unfit
house.

The drawback to the current definition of unfitness is that it
is often difficult to distinguish the criteria for houses which are
in need of repair or rehabilitation and those which should be
immediately closed. A more realistic standard for closure, and
thus one which is more likely to be treated seriously, might be
based on the original conception of immediate risk of injury to
the health or well-being of the occupants under the Public
Health Acts rather than the current conception of suitability
for occupation under the Housing Acts. In this way the designation of houses for immediate closure in the interests of the
occupants could be distinguished from the longer term
concerns in respect of standards of repair and possible rehabilitation or renewal which should be dealt with through the
proposed repair and rehabilitation procedures.

The procedure for dealing with houses deemed to fall below
the closing standard should be designed accordingly to secure
immediate action. Local authorities should be required to
serve a closing notice on the owner of any such house. The
owner should then be allowed a brief period of up to two weeks

to make representations to the local authority or to enter an appeal on the ground that the accommodation did not fall below the standard. The local authority might be permitted to accept an undertaking from the owner to bring the house above the closing standard within a specified period of up to perhaps three months. But if such an undertaking was not made or was so impractical as to be unlikely to be carried out, the local authority should be required to issue an immediate closing order and to rehouse the occupants. Neither the owner nor the local authority would then be permitted to use the house until it had been brought above the closing standard, and in the case of rented accommodation the local authority would then be entitled to nominate a replacement for any person who had been rehoused. The future of the house could then be solved by the standard procedures for voluntary or compulsory rehabilitation by the owner or voluntary or compulsory purchase by the local authority, whether for rehabilitation or demolition and renewal.

Compulsory purchase and powers of entry

The principal drawback to the current law on compulsory purchase and entry, like that of most other aspects of housing law, is its complexity. A strong case may be made for the simplification of the various concurrent provisions under which local authorities may acquire land and houses for rehabilitation or renewal. The most appropriate general formulation for this purpose, given the way in which these powers are actually used, might be to authorise the initiation of a CPO in any case where the local authority can show that a higher standard of accommodation or management, or the same standard at lower cost to tenants or taxpayers, would thereby be attained. In addition, as already suggested, local authorities should be permitted to proceed to the immediate compulsory purchase of those houses in which they have carried out substantial works of rehabilitation in default, without having to wait for ministerial confirmation of a CPO. This would mean that, as in the case of purchase notices, the work of rehabilitation could proceed without the lengthy delays required for the processing of a CPO under current procedures. In cases where this expedited power of purchase and entry is not available local authorities might usefully be granted a more effective power to control the termination of existing tenancies or the creation of new ones in the period between the initiation of a CPO and its final confirmation by the Department of the Environment.

A new housing court or tribunal

These proposed procedures could readily be administered within the existing court structure. There would be a considerable advantage, however, if the administration of all aspects of housing law could be brought together in a single court or tribunal. Under the existing law, as already described, three sets of courts and tribunals are directly involved in adjudications and appeals. The principal forum for dealing with matters arising out of the administration of the Housing Acts is the county court, which also deals with security of tenure and certain other matters under the Rent Acts. The fixing of fair rents, however, is dealt with by a separate structure comprising rent officers, rent assessment committees and rent tribunals (see Andrew Arden, *Housing: Security and Rent Control*). Most matters arising under the Public Health Acts are dealt with by local magistrates courts. The recommendations which have been made to link the fixing of reasonable rents with procedures for enforcing repair and rehabilitation notices through reasonable expense criteria suggest that all these different jurisdictions should be combined. This would enable the same court or tribunal to deal at the same time with disputes over the assessment of a fair rent, the extent of the repair or rehabilitation which could reasonably be required within the reasonable expense criterion, and the security of tenure or rehousing of the occupants. From the point of view of local authorities this would assist in streamlining the administration of the various parts of housing law currently divided between Environmental Health and Housing Departments. And from the point of view of tenants, whether in the public or private sector, it would greatly simplify the procedural problems in enforcing their rights in relation to rent, repair obligations and security of tenure. It would also be possible to bring in competent assessors on technical issues of housing standards and valuation to assist in resolving disputes over repair and rehabilitation notices as well as in the fixing of fair rents under existing structures. Given the complexity of many of the issues involved in housing law it would seem appropriate to centre a new housing court or tribunal on the existing county courts rather than on magistrates courts, and to provide for technical assessors to sit with the judge in appropriate cases.

Housing law and housing policy

It has not been the purpose of this book to argue a case for any particular approach to matters of housing policy or housing finance, whether in respect of levels of grant aid, the balance between area rehabilitation programmes and action in respect of individual houses on a more general basis, or the broader issue of the extent to which further encouragement should be given to the private rented sector or to municipalisation. Policies on all these matters may be expected to change from time to time at both national and local levels. The purpose of the integrated code which has been proposed is simply to provide a coherent and effective legal framework within which any or all of the various policy options may be pursued. The distinction between matters of law and matters of policy which this suggests is not of course precise or absolute. But it is not unreasonable to suggest that more could be achieved with less unnecessary administrative effort if the distinction between the creation of a basic legal framework of the kind proposed and the implementation of specific policies were more widely recognised.

Appendix A: Model Tenancy Agreements

1. The respective duties of landlord and tenant in respect of maintenance and repair under the National Consumer Council Model Tenancy Agreement

This tenancy agreement was designed primarily for local authority housing and covers all aspects of the landlord/tenant relationship. The clauses dealing with maintenance and repair, with suitable amendments, might be used as the basis of private sector and housing association tenancies. The full Model Tenancy Agreement is published as an appendix to *Tenancy Agreements between councils and their tenants* (National Consumer Council, 1976).

Obligations of the Tenant

The tenant shall:

Rent

    (1) Pay the rent regularly and promptly.

Repairs

    (2) Repair or replace items damaged through the neglect or carelessness of the tenant or his/her household.

Decoration

    (3) Keep the interor of the dwelling in a reasonable state of decoration.

Access

    (4) Allow officers of the council to enter the premises after receiving 24 hours written notice of the morning or afternoon of the visit, and on production of a pass, for the purpose of inspecting the state of repair of the dwelling or carrying out repairs.

End of tenancy

  (5) At the end of the tenancy, leave the dwelling and the council's fixtures and fittings in the same state as they were at the beginning of the tenancy, fair wear and tear and landlord's failure to carry out his obligations excepted.

The tenant shall not without the council's written permission, which shall not be unreasonably withheld:

  ...

  (3) Carry out structural alterations or make additions to the premises including fixtures such as new fireplaces, immersion heaters, sinks, wiring, etc.
  (4) Decorate the exterior of the premises.

Obligations of the Landlord

The council shall:

Repairs of structure and exterior

  (1) Keep in good repair the structure and exterior of the premises, including:
  (a) drains, gutters and external pipes;
  (b) the roof;
  (c) outside walls, outside doors, windowsills, window catches, sash cords, glazing putties and window frames and glass — including necessary painting and decoration;
  (d) internal walls, skirting boards, doors and door frames, hinges, locks, door jambs, thresholds, letter boxes, door handles, floors and ceilings — not including painting and decoration;
  (e) chimneys and chimney stacks — this does not include the sweeping of house chimneys but does include sweeping the chimneys of flats;
  (f) pathways, steps or other means of access;
  (g) plasterwork.

The council will not be liable for the repair of any of the above if such repair becomes necessary through the fault of the tenant.

Repair of installations

  (2) Keep in good repair and working order the installa-
      tions for space heating, water heating and sanitation
      and for the supply of water, gas and electricity,
      including:
      (a) basins, sinks, baths, toilets, flushing systems and
          waste pipes;
      (b) electric wiring, gas pipes and water pipes;
      (c) water heaters, fireplaces and fitted fires;
      (d) sockets and light fittings.

The council will only be liable to repair the above if they fall
out of repair through no fault of the tenant and also provided
they were not fitted by the present tenant without the council's
written consent. In addition the council undertakes to replace
any of the above if they do not function efficiently because of
faulty design, provided they were part of the premises at the
commencement of the tenancy.

Repair of communal parts in flats

  (3) In the case of flats, the council shall take reasonable
      care to keep the common entrances, halls, stairways,
      lifts, passageways, rubbish chutes and any other
      common parts in reasonable repair and safe and fit
      for use by the tenants, their families and visitors.
      This includes a duty to keep in reasonable repair the
      lighting of common parts.

External decoration

  (4) Decorate the exterior of all houses and flats as and
      when necessary or at least once every seven years
      unless the tenant wishes to carry out external decora-
      tion himself in which case permission shall not be
      unreasonably withheld.

Decoration of communal parts

  (5) Decorate communal areas of blocks of flats as and
      when necessary or at least once every three years.

Internal decoration

    (6) Decorate the interior and tend the gardens of premises if the tenant is unable to do so because of age or handicap and if no other member of the tenant's household is able to do so.

Access

    (7) Give 24 hours written notice of the morning or afternoon of any visit for the purpose of inspecting the state of repair of the dwelling or carrying out repairs.

Remedies Available to the Tenant if the Council Fails to Comply with the Agreement

Non-urgent repairs

In the event of the council failing to carry out a non-urgent repair for which it is responsible (such as perished plasterwork, broken sash cords, general disrepair and maintenance) within five weeks of notification to them in writing or by personal visit of the tenant, the tenant may carry out the necessary work at reasonable expense, and having notified the council of the amount may withhold rent to that amount.

Urgent repairs

In the event of the council failing to carry out urgent repairs (such as collapsed floors, collapsing ceiling plaster, holed roofs, damaged doors, broken glazing), within nine days of notification to them in writing or by personal visit of the tenant, the tenant may carry out the necessary work at reasonable expense, and having notified the council of the amount may withhold rent to that amount.

Extremely urgent repairs

In the event of the council failing to repair or remedy the failure of the water supply, the disconnection of gas or electricity through damage to the fittings, or blocked drains, within 48 hours of notification to them in writing or by personal visit of the tenant, the tenant may carry out the necessary work at reasonable expense, and having notified the council of the amount may withhold rent to that amount.

Legal remedies

If the council fails to carry out repairs for which it is responsible, and the tenant either cannot afford to or is not prepared to do them himself, the tenant is not prevented by anything in this agreement from seeking legal redress.

Supply of heat or hot water

If any supply of heating and/or hot water provided by the council should fail for a period exceeding 48 hours the council shall, on the application of the tenant, allow him an appropriate rebate in rent. This will not prevent the tenant from claiming any other legal remedy.

Failure to keep appointments

In the event of council workmen failing to keep an appointment to gain access to the dwelling, the council shall, on the application of the tenant, compensate him for any loss of earnings incurred, for which the tenant must produce proof.

Further Remedies Available to the Tenant in Law

Defects that are prejudicial to health

If a tenant informs the council of defects in his dwelling which are prejudicial to health, and the council fails to remedy the defects, the tenant may apply to the magistrate's court for a summons under section 99 of the Public Health Act 1936 ordering the council to remedy the defects.

Outstanding repairs

Under section 125 of the Housing Act 1974 the tenant has the right to ask the county court for an order that any outstanding repair that is the landlord's responsibility be carried out. The tenant can also claim damages.

Unfit premises

A tenant has the right to claim to a justice of the peace that his house is unfit for human habitation under section 157(2) and section 4 of the Housing Act 1957. The council must take action on unfit premises.

Remedies Available to the Council if the Tenant Fails to Comply with the Agreement

Tenant's repairs

The council may notify the tenant in writing of repairs he must carry out within a period specified in the notice, and in the event of the tenant failing to carry out the necessary work the council may enter the premises, do the necessary work and charge the tenant a reasonable sum for it.

2. *A model Agreement for Tenants to Carry Out Their Own Repairs*

This model agreement is designed primarily for a house or a group of flats whose tenants are willing to take responsibility for regular maintenance and repair in return for a regular abatement of rent. Since the landlord retains residual responsibility for major repairs which cannot be paid for by an abatement of rent it is probably not necessary for the agreement to be approved in advance by a county court under section 32(6) of the Housing Act 1961, though it would be safer if any legal enforcement is envisaged to submit it for approval. Similar principles may be applied, with suitable amendment to individual tenancies.

This agreement is made between . . . . (the landlord) and the following tenants of flats at 123 Reasonable Street, Easthampton

Flat 1 . . . . , ...

Flat 2 . . . .

Flat 3 . . . .

(1) The tenants shall deduct ten per cent (10%) from their monthly rent and pay it into a communal repair fund; they shall maintain for this purpose a joint bank

account on which cheques may be drawn by any two signatories.

(2) The tenants shall be responsible for making payments from the repair fund for any necessary maintenance and repair both in individual flats and in common parts of the premises; payments may be made either to independent contractors or to individual tenants who carry out their own repairs.

(3) At the end of each accounting year the tenants shall give an account to the landlord of all payments into and expenditure from the repair fund and of any balance remaining in the fund.

(4) Any surplus in the repair fund at the end of an accounting year shall be carried forward; if at any time the amount of the repair fund is in excess of ten per cent of the annual rents payable by the tenants, the excess may be spent on improvements and replacements and shall be allocated in an equitable manner between individual tenants.

(5) If the repair fund is at any time insufficient to meet the full cost of any repairs which the landlord is obliged to carry out under section 32 of the Housing Act 1961, the tenants shall give notice to the landlord of the additional amount required to meet the full cost, and if the landlord does not object may deduct that amount from current rents and pay it into the repair fund; the landlord may on receipt of a notice under this clause take control of the necessary repairs and may draw on the repair fund for that purpose.

(6) Any dispute under this agreement may be referred to arbitration by any person chosen with the consent of both the landlord and the tenants.

(7) This agreement may be terminated by the landlord or by any or all of the tenants by one month's notice in writing; on termination the balance in the repair fund, or any relevant proportion of the balance, shall be paid to the landlord.

Signed . . . . (landlord)

. . . . (tenant)

Appendix B: Obtaining a Landlord's Address

1. *Model Letter to Rent Collector Requiring Disclosure of the Name and Address of a Landlord*

This letter is intended to be used when a less formal request, whether orally or in writing, has been rejected or ignored. The letter should be sent by recorded delivery to the person to whom rent is paid. Several copies should be retained in case it becomes necessary to ask the local authority or the police to take criminal proceedings for a breach of section 121 of the Housing Act 1974 which requires rent collectors to provide the name and address of landlords.

Flat 3
321 Awful Street
Westhampton
September 31, 1979

Dear Mr Collector,

   I am writing formally to ask you, as the person to whom I pay rent in respect of the above flat, to let me know the full name and address of my landlord. As you may know you are obliged to give me this information by section 121 of the Housing Act 1974, and it is a criminal offence not to comply. If I do not hear from you in writing within the next seven days, I shall be forced to draw the attention of the local authority and the police to your lack of co-operation in this matter.

Yours faithfully,
John Tenant

2.   *Obtaining the Address of a Company*

Where the landlord is a company, it may be necessary to obtain the address of its registered office for the service of any formal legal documents. This may be obtained free of charge by telephoning Companies House in Cardiff (0222 388588) and giving the full name of the company, or its registered number, which should appear on all correspondence of the company. Alternatively a personal visit may be made to Companies House in Cardiff or in London (55 City Road, London EC1). If a personal visit is not possible a private company search agency may be employed at a cost of a few pounds. The names and addresses of such search agencies may be found in the telephone directory under the general heading "Company." Companies House does *not* now deal with written applications.

Appendix C: Suing a Landlord for Breach of a Duty to Repair

Model Particulars of Claim in Respect of a Breach by a Landlord of the Statutory Repairing Covenants under Section 32 of the Housing Act 1961

This model particulars of claim is intended for use by tenants who wish to take legal action against their landlord to enforce the repairing covenants under section 32 of the Housing Act 1961 (see Chapter 3). It may be varied to cover the enforcement of non-statutory covenants by deleting any reference to the Housing Act 1961 and referring instead to the relevant clause of a written tenancy agreement or to an implied term. The particulars of claim should be taken to the office of the local county court, where a fee of between £5 and £15 will be payable (recoverable if the case is successful). The tenant will also have to fill in a request form asking for the service of a summons on the landlord by a court official, for which there is an additional fee of £2. The model includes both a claim for specific performance, *i.e.* a court order for the landlord to carry out the necessary repairs, and a separate claim for damages for the period for which the repairs have remained undone. Either of these may be omitted. If the landlord is a limited company, as in the model, the tenant must ensure that the company's name is accurately stated, and the summons should normally be served at the company's registered office. If the defendant is an individual, his or her full name should be given and the summons should be served at his or her usual address.

In the Westhampton County Court	Plaint No. ...
Between John Tenant	*Plaintiff*
and	
Landlord Ltd.	*Defendant*

(1) The plaintiff is a tenant of the defendant at Flat 3, 321 Awful Street, Westhampton, and pays a weekly rent of £8.

(2) The rateable value of the flat is less than £1,500.

(3) The ceiling of the front bedroom in the flat is defective and several small pieces of plaster have fallen from it.

(4) The defendant has a duty to repair the ceiling under section 32 of the Housing Act 1961.

(5) On 31 November 1979 the plaintiff requested the defendant to carry out the necessary repairs.

(6) The defendant has failed to carry out the necessary repairs.

(7) The plaintiff claims an order for specific performance under section 125 of the Housing Act 1974.

(8) The plaintiff also claims damages of £5, being £1 for each week for which the repairs have remained undone since the landlord was informed, and costs.

Appendix D: Self-Help Repairs

These letters are intended for use by tenants who are prepared to undertake repairs for which the landlord is legally responsible and to deduct the cost from the rent. It is important to complete each of the various steps set out in Chapter 3 before embarking on such repairs, and to retain copies of each letter sent and of all invoices for materials and work done. These model letters assume that a contractor or independent workman will be employed; though there is no reason in strict law why a tenant should not charge for his own labour as well as for materials, it would be wise in such cases to obtain a quotation from an independent contractor or an independent assessment of the value of the work done.

1. *First Letter to Landlord (Notice of Defect)*

Flat 3,
321 Awful Street,
Westhampton
November 31, 1979

Dear Sir,
    I am writing to inform you that the ceiling of the front bedroom in the above flat is defective and that small pieces of plaster have been falling from it. I should be grateful if you would arrange for the necessary repairs to be carried out as soon as possible. As you will know you are obliged to carry out this work under section 32 of the Housing Act 1961.

Yours faithfully,
John Tenant

2. *Second Letter to Landlord (Notice of Intention to Carry out Repairs)*

Flat 3,
321 Awful Street,
Westhampton
December 15, 1979

Dear Sir,

I wrote to you on November 31, 1979 about the defective ceiling in the front bedroom in the above flat. As you have not taken any action to carry out the necessary repairs I propose to have the work carried out myself and to deduct the cost from the rent. If by December 22 I have not received from you a written undertaking that you will carry out the work before the end of the month, I shall instruct a contractor to carry out the necessary repairs to make the ceiling safe. I shall pay the contractor myself, and then deduct the full amount of his invoice, of which I shall send you a copy, from the rent which I owe you, starting from the week after the completion of the work. I hope this arrangement will be acceptable to you, though I should add that I have a recognised legal right to act in this way.

Yours faithfully,
John Tenant

Appendix E: Initiating the Statutory Nuisance Procedure

These model letters and forms are intended for those who wish to initiate the statutory nuisance procedure under section 99 of the Public Health Act 1936. The models are drafted for use by the tenant of a private landlord in cases where the local Environmental Health Department is unwilling to take proceedings on its own account. They may readily be amended for use by council tenants. Though it is not strictly necessary it is wise to begin by sending a formal letter both to the landlord and to the local Environmental Health Department asking for action to be taken to remedy the nuisance. If these letters do not produce the desired effect, the tenant should then prepare a formal *information* and a *statement of informant* along the lines of the models and take them to the office of the Clerk to the Justices (*i.e.* the office of the local Magistrates Court), which will be found in the Telephone Directory under "Courts."

1. Letter to Landlord (*Notice of Defect*)

Flat 3,
321 Awful Street,
Westhampton
November 31, 1979

Landlord Ltd.,
Property House,
Main Street,
Westhampton.

Dear Sir,

I am writing to draw your attention to the condition of the above premises, and in particular to the following items:

1. Defective ceiling in front bedroom;
2. Defective downspouting on rear wall, causing dampness in rear bedroom.

It is my opinion that these defects constitute a statutory nuisance under section 92 of the Public Health Act 1936. I am writing today to the Environmental Health Department to request an inspection of the premises for that purpose. I hope that you will be able to deal with these defects, for which you are responsible under the terms of my tenancy, so that further proceedings need not be taken.

Yours faithfully,
John Tenant

2. *Letter to Environmental Health Department*

Flat 3,
321 Awful Street,
Westhampton.
November 31, 1979

Chief Environmental Health Officer,
Westhampton District Council.

Dear Sir,

Flat 3, 321 Awful Street, Westhampton

I am writing to make a formal complaint about the condition of the above premises, of which I am a weekly tenant, and in particular about the following items:

1. Defective ceiling in front bedroom.
2. Defective downspouting on rear wall, causing dampness in rear bedroom.

I feel that these defects may constitute a statutory nuisance. I should therefore be grateful if you could arrange for one of your officers to make an inspection of the premises and for any necessary action to be taken to remedy the situation. I shall be in all afternoon on Thursday December 5; if that time is not suitable, please send me a letter stating when your officer will call so that I may make arrangements for someone to be here to let him in.

Yours faithfully,
John Tenant

3. *Model information under section 99 of the Public Health Act 1936*

In the Westhampton Magistrates' Court

December 15, 1979
Accused: Landlord Ltd
Address: 123 Property Buildings, Main Street, Westhampton

Alleged offence: Breach of section 92 of the Public Health Act 1936
The information of John Tenant
Flat 3, 321 Awful Street, Westhampton
who upon oath states that the accused committed the offence of which particulars are given in the attached statement.

Signed: .... (Justice of the Peace)
.... (Clerk to the Justices)

4. *Model Statement of Informant Under Section 99 of the Public Health Act 1936*

Statement of Informant

Name: John Tenant
Address: Flat 3, 321 Awful Street, Westhampton
Occupation: Shop assistant
Age: 35

I am the occupier of Flat 3, 321 Awful Street, Westhampton

My landlord is Landlord Ltd., Property Buildings, Main Street, Westhampton

The premises occupied by me are a statutory nuisance under section 92 of the Public Health Act

1936 due to the following defects:
1. Defective ceiling in front bedroom.
2. Defective downspouting on rear wall, causing dampness in rear bedroom.

The premises have been in a bad state of repair since September 1979, and on November 31, 1979 I informed the accused in writing of the defects, for which he is responsible under the terms of my tenancy. The accused has failed to remedy the defects.

In these circumstances I request the court to grant me a summons against the accused.

Signed: ....
John Tenant

Appendix F: Initiating the Unfitness Procedures Under the Housing Act 1957

These model letters are intended for use by the occupants of accommodation which is in worse condition than can readily be dealt with by straightforward repairs. The result of having a dwelling declared to be unfit is more likely to be a closing order and temporary or permanent rehousing by the local authority than effective action to have it made fit (see Chapter 4). The procedure should thus be used only by those who are anxious or willing to be rehoused. The first step is to have a survey made of the condition of the dwelling, and to prepare a report listing all the defects in each part of it, both inside and outside. A letter and a copy of the report should then be sent to the Environmental Health Department asking for the dwelling to be inspected to see whether it is unfit. If this does not produce the desired result, a formal complaint may then be made to a justice of the peace, asking him to require the local authority to determine whether the dwelling is unfit under section 157 of the Housing Act 1957. A copy of the report should be attached to the complaint. A model complaint from the justice of the peace to the local authority is provided. It is also desirable, though not strictly necessary, to inform the owner of the dwelling that an application for a fitness inspection is being made.

1. *Letter to Local Authority Asking for a Fitness Inspection*

Flat 3,
321 Awful Street,
Westhampton.
November 31, 1979

Chief Environmental Health Officer,
Westhampton District Council,

Dear Sir,

Flat 3, 321 Awful Street, Westhampton

I am writing to inform you of the condition of the above premises of which I am a weekly tenant. On the basis of the enclosed report, I feel that the dwelling may be unfit for human habitation under section 4 of the Housing Act 1957. I should therefore be grateful if you could arrange for one of your officers to make an inspection and to determine whether or not the dwelling is unfit. I shall be in all afternoon on Thursday, December 5; if that time is not suitable, please send me a letter stating when your officer will call so that I may make arrangements for someone to be here to let him in.

Yours faithfully,
John Tenant

2. *Model Letter to a Justice of the Peace Requesting Action under Section 157 of the Housing Act 1957*

Flat 3,
321 Awful Street,
Westhampton.
December 15, 1979

Albert Booth, Esq.,
Justice of the Peace for the District of Westhampton.

Dear Sir,

I am writing to inform you of the condition of my dwelling at the above address. On the basis of the enclosed report, I feel that the dwelling may be unfit for human habitation under section 4 of the Housing Act 1957.

I notified the Westhampton District Council of the condition of the premises on November 31, 1979, but the Council has failed to make a determination as to whether the dwelling is unfit.

I am therefore requesting you, as a justice of the peace, to make a complaint in writing to the Westhampton District Council as provided under section 157(2) of the Housing Act 1957 (as amended by Schedule 29, para. 4 of the Local Government Act 1972) requiring them forthwith to have an inspection of the dwelling made and a report submitted to the Council on its condition so that the Council may decide whether it should be dealt with as unfit for human habitation under the Housing Acts.

Yours faithfully,
John Tenant

3. *Model Complaint from Justice of the Peace to Local Authority*

The Chief Executive Officer,
Westhampton District Council,
Town Hall, Westhampton.

Flat 3, 321 Awful Street, Westhampton

I, Albert Booth, Justice of the Peace for the Westhampton District, hereby make a complaint under section 157(2) of the Housing Act 1957 (as amended by Schedule 29, para. 4 of the Local Government Act 1972), being satisfied that the above dwelling is unfit for human habitation under section 4 of the Housing Act 1957, and request that the Council forthwith have an inspection of the dwelling made and a recommendation submitted to the Council as to whether it should be dealt with as unfit for human habitation under the Housing Acts.

Signed:

Albert Booth, Justice of the Peace

Date: December 15, 1979

Appendix G: Initiating a Compulsory Improvement Notice

Compulsory improvement notices, requiring a landlord to install a bathroom or other facilities along with necessary repairs, cannot be served by a local authority without a formal request from a tenant, unless the dwelling is in a GIA or HAA. This letter is intended primarily for use by such tenants. It may also be used by tenants within GIAs and HAAs, though it is not strictly necessary. Though a local authority is not bound to carry through the compulsory improvement procedures, either in GIAs or HAAs or elsewhere, it is more likely to do so if a formal request is made; even if it decides against serving a compulsory improvement notice, it may well feel obliged to take some other action to improve conditions. The letter may be sent either to the Chief Environmental Health Officer or to the Chief Executive/Town Clerk.

Flat 4,
321 Awful Street,
Westhampton.
Westhampton.
September 31, 1979

The Chief Environmental Health Officer,
Westhampton District Council.

Dear Sir,

Flat 4, 321 Awful Street, Westhampton

I am writing to ask your assistance in securing the provision of facilities in my dwelling. The dwelling was built before 1961 and lacks the following items from the list of standard amenities:

	Available	Not available
A fixed bath or shower.		
A supply of hot and cold water to a fixed bath or shower		

A supply of hot and cold
water to a wash-hand basin.
A sink.
A supply of hot and cold
water to a sink.
A W.C. within or readily
accessible from the dwelling.

I should be grateful if you could arrange to have the premises inspected with a view to serving a compulsory improvement notice under Part VIII of the Housing Act 1974 on my landlord, who has repeatedly refused to install the missing facilities. The landlord is Landlord Ltd., Property House, High Street, Westhampton. I shall be in all afternoon on Thursday October 5; if that time is not suitable please send me a letter stating when your officer will call so that I may make arrangements for someone to be here to let him in.

Yours faithfully,
John Tenant

Appendix H: Improvement Grants

The following list of items for which an improvement grant may be made is based on a survey of 77 local authorities carried out for the Consumer Association and published in *Which?* in July 1976. The items included are those which the local authorities reported that they would in appropriate circumstances be prepared to treat as *improvements* as opposed to *repairs*, and thus as eligible for an improvement grant. Once a substantial item of improvement has been identified, repairs costing an equivalent amount may also be grant aided. But the final decision on what constitutes an improvement and on whether an improvement grant should be made rests with the local authority, which has discretion to refuse any application.

1. All standard amenities for which you can get an intermediate grant (bath or shower, wash-hand basin, sink, hot and cold water supply and an accessible W.C.) provided other work is carried out.

2. Damp-proof course in walls and floors; stopping damp penetration if no cavity in wall.

3. Replacing rotten wooden or damp floors with solid damp-proof floors; reducing ground level to 150mm below damp-proof course; underfloor ventilation; strengthening foundations because original foundations were inadequate.

4. Installation of electric or gas lighting and electric power points; installation of electricity supply (or bottled gas, if no electricity); laying a gas supply (but only the part within the property).

5. Replacing shallow or obsolete kitchen sink with modern sink unit; putting in a U-bend if there isn't one.

6. Fitting handrail on stairs; replacing steep and winding

staircase with straight one; installing two-way switch for staircase light.

7. Space for storage and preparation of food; making ventilated lobby between W.C. and kitchen or living room.

8. Putting in partition walls to give direct access (*e.g.* from a landing) to bedrooms and bathroom.

9. Increasing ceiling height to about 2.3m or more; increasing door height to 2m or more; strengthening single brick walls.

10. Access to roof space; party wall between ceiling and roof to increase sound insulation and provide fire protection.

11. Increasing adequate living or kitchen area by removing disused fireplace, chimney breast or cooking range, or by rearranging room by knocking down internal walls; extending home to increase kitchen area; bricking up defective fireplace.

12. Putting roofing felt between tiles and rafters.

13. Putting in addition windows or enlarging small ones; putting in extractor fan where installing windows not possible; fitting glass door to give natural light to hall, staircase, landing etc.

14. Central heating if part of comprehensive improvement (but not in bedroom); lagging tanks and pipes; fixed electric, gas or oil heaters; provision of satisfactory fuel store; replacing obsolete fireplaces with approved fireplaces; lining old chimney flues.

15. Installing gutters and drainpipes and connection to drains; making the front door watertight; provision of grooved windowsill where previously none existed.

16. Taking down bulging brickwork and rebuilding.

17. Second W.C. if existing one can be reached only through a bedroom.

18. Adapting basement rooms to modern regulations.

19. Path to front and back doors; paved areas adjoining home.

20. Insulating walls (especially to cure condensation).

21. Provision of adequate drainage, *i.e.* mains or cesspool or septic tank where no main drainage exists.

22. Redecoration made necessary by improvements, but not general redecoration; plaster on walls or ceilings not previously plastered.

23. All work necessary to comply with fire regulations.
24. All work connected with converting a house into flats.
25. Fees to architect or building adviser for work for which you get a grant.

Additional Items Which Might be Treated as Improvements in Certain Cases

26. Damp-proof course which needs to be replaced (and rotten wood treated) because it was not installed properly.
27. Replacement of a bath without an overflow.
28. Replacement of a corrugated iron or lightweight asbestos cement roof with heavier material.

Appendix I: Overcrowding

The statutory definition of overcrowding contained in section 77 of the Housing Act 1957 is as follows:

77. — (1) A dwelling-house shall be deemed for the purposes of this Act to be overcrowded at any time when the number of persons sleeping in the house either —

(a) is such that any two of those persons, being persons ten years old or more of opposite sexes and not being persons living together as husband and wife, must sleep in the same room; or

(b) is, in relation to the number and floor area of the rooms of which the house consists, in excess of the permitted number of persons as defined in the Sixth Schedule to this Act.

(2) In determining for the purposes of this section the number of persons sleeping in a house, no account shall be taken of a child under one year old, and a child who has attained one year and is under ten years old shall be reckoned as one-half of a unit.

SIXTH SCHEDULE

Number of Persons Permitted to Use a House for Sleeping

For the purposes of Part IV of this Act, the expression "the permitted number of persons" means, in relation to any dwelling-house, either —

(a) the number specified in the second column of Table I in the annex hereto in relation to a house consisting of the number of rooms of which that house consists, or

(*b*) the aggregate for all the rooms in the house
obtained by reckoning, for each room therein
of the floor area specified in the first column of
Table II in the annex hereto, the number specified in the second column of that Table in
relation to that area,

whichever is the less:

Providing that in computing for the purposes of the
said Table I the number of rooms in a house, no regard
shall be had to any room having a floor area of less than
50 square feet.

Annex

Table I

Where a house consists of:
(*a*)	One room	2
(*b*)	Two rooms	3
(*c*)	Three rooms	5
(*d*)	Four rooms	7½
(*e*)	Five rooms or more	10, with an additional 2 in respect of each room in excess of five.

Table II

Where the floor area of a room is:
(*a*)	110 sq. ft. or more	2
(*b*)	90 sq. ft. or more, but less than 110 sq. ft.	1½
(*c*)	70 sq. ft. or more, but less than 90 sq. ft.	1
(*d*)	50 sq. ft. or more, but less than 70 sq. ft.	½
(*e*)	Under 50 sq. ft.	Nil

Appendix J: The Reasonable Expense Criterion

1. *The Purpose of the Criterion*

The purpose of a reasonable expense criterion is to impose some limit on the repairs which a local authority may require owners or landlords to carry out. There are currently three statutory formulations. For the purpose of repair notices under section 9(1) of the Housing Act 1957 in respect of unfit houses reasonable expense is directly linked to the relationship between the cost of the works and the value of the property. For the purpose of compulsory improvement notices under Part VIII of the Housing Act 1974 the criterion is also that of reasonable expense, but there is no statutory requirement that the cost of the repairs should be compared with the value of the house. For the purpose of repair notices under section 9 (1A) of the Housing Act 1957 in respect of houses which are fit but in substantial disrepair there is no reference to reasonable expense as such but the repairs prescribed must be reasonable in relation to the age, character and locality of the house. In interpreting these various provisions the courts have adopted essentially the same approach, that owners should not be forced to carry out works which are uneconomic in the sense of costing more than the resulting increase in the value of the property. The main difficulty has been in finding an appropriate practical formula which may be applied in all cases.

2. *The Reasonable Expense Criterion under the Housing Act 1957, s. 9(1)*

The reasonable expense criterion was first introduced in the Housing Act 1930 to limit the power given to local authorities to require owners to make unfit houses fit. The only guidance to the application of the criterion was the formal provision, re-enacted under section 39 of the Housing Act 1957, that "in determining ... whether a house can be rendered fit for human habitation at reasonable expense, regard shall be had to the estimated cost of the works necessary to render it so fit and the value which it is estimated to have when the works are completed."

The practical application of the criterion soon gave rise to difficulty, and there was considerable uncertainty both among local authorities and in official reports on how it should be administered. There was also wide variation in the approach of county courts in cases taken on appeal. In one study it was shown that the ratio of costs to the valuation of the property varied from 33 per cent to 83 per cent in cases judged to be of reasonable expense, and from 27 per cent to 166 per cent in cases judged to be of unreasonable expense (see N. Skedge, *Houses and their repair with special emphasis on the subject of reasonable expense*, Association of Public Health Inspectors Monograph Series, 1973). Crude figures like these, however, conceal some important principles which have been established in the higher courts. In the first place it has been decided that the reasonableness of the expense must be judged by its impact on the owner, rather than at large; accordingly any grant which may be payable towards the cost of the prescribed works must be taken into account:

Harrington v. *Croydon Corporation (1966)*

An improvement notice was served on the owner of a tenanted three-bedroomed terrace house, requiring the provision of a bathroom extension costed at £650; the house was valued at investment value, with a sitting tenant, at £410 or £550 unimproved and £750 or £1,075 improved by the owner's and local authority valuers respectively; a grant of 50 per cent was payable on the prescribed works; it was held that reasonable expense for the purposes of the Housing Act 1964 meant reasonable expense to those called upon to bear it, and that in determining whether the expense which the owner was called upon to bear was reasonable, the grant and the addition which the owner would be entitled to make to the tenant's rent should be taken into account; it was not unreasonable for an owner to be required to spend £325 on improvements which would increase the capital value of the property by either £340 or £525 on the respective valuations, given that the owner was entitled to a gross return on the money spent of 12½ per cent by way of an increase in the controlled rent.

It has also been established that the date for assessing reasonable expense is that of the court hearing (*Leslie Morris & Co. Ltd.* v. *Willesden Corporation* (1953). In practice this means that if there is any substantial delay between the initiation of proceedings and the hearing of any appeal the calculations of costs and valuations and any allowable grant aid should be redone to take account of inflation. It is not necessary, however, for detailed and accurate figures to be prepared before any repair notice is served:

> *Cohen* v. *West Ham Corporation (1923)*
> A local authority served notices on the owner of a number of unfit houses requiring him to make them fit. The owner objected on the ground that the council had not properly considered whether the works prescribed could be carried out at reasonable expense since it had relied on the recommendation of its officers. It was held on appeal that unless there was evidence to the contrary the courts would not assume that a council had not carried out its duty in this respect: "(the Act) does not require that there should be a close examination ... before the initiative is taken; ... the local authority may take into account not merely an accurate estimate made by a surveyor or an estate agent with a schedule of dilapidations but ... what would probably be the cost of the outlay required ... "

This does not mean that notices may properly be served without any consideration of costs in relation to the reasonable expense criterion, but that a local authority may set the procedures in motion on the basis of simple calculations of average costs and values by the officers concerned.

It has been confirmed in two more recent decisions that the proper method of assessing whether the cost to the owner of prescribed works is reasonable or unreasonable is to compare the valuation of the property before and after the completion of the works:

Kimsey v. *Barnet London Borough Council (1976)*
A local authority served a notice on the owner of a
maisonette which was agreed to be unfit, requiring substantial works costed at £2,062 to render it fit; the owner
argued that the works necessary to make the premises fit
would cost some £3,500. The local authority and the
owner valued the premises with a sitting tenant after the
completion of the works at £2,700 and £2,750 respectively. The Court of Appeal accepted the County Court
judge's findings that the necessary works would cost something over £2,000, and that the value subject to the
tenancy on completion of the works would be £2,700; on
the basis that the value of an unfit maisonette which
could not be demolished, since it was required to provide
support for a fit maisonette upstairs, was nil, it was held
that the works could be carried out at reasonable expense:
"one looks first to see what would be the value of the
property at the end of the day when the necessary works
to render the property fit have been carried out; ... one
then deducts from that any existing value which is
properly attributable to the premises in their present
state; and finally one asks 'Is the difference between the
two figures greater or less than the cost of repairs?',"
subject only to an allowance for the fact that instalments
may have to be paid to a builder before the property can
be let out again on completion of the works.

Ellis Copp & Co. v. *London Borough of*
Richmond-upon-Thames (1976)
A local authority served a notice on the owner of an unfit
tenanted house requiring works costed at £4,000 to render
it fit; there were widely varying views on the valuation of
the property before and after the completion of these
works, but the County Court judge found that the value
before the works could be put at £2,000 and the value
after at £6,000 subject to the tenancy, and held that the
works could therefore be done at reasonable expense. In
the Court of Appeal it was held that on the evidence the
cost of the works, including decoration, should have
been fixed at more than £5,000, and that in addition
the cost to the owner of borrowing the money to carry
out the works at 18 per cent interest would be greater than
the permissible increase in rental income of 12½ per

cent; the judge should have concluded that the house could not be made fit at reasonable expense, and the notice was accordingly quashed.

It has also been confirmed that the proper basis for valuation of properties for this purpose is the open market value:

Inworth Property Co. v. *London Borough of Southwark (1977)*

A local authority served a notice on the owner of an unfit house requiring works costed at £1,800 to render it fit; it was agreed that the value of the property before the works was £1,300 on the open market and that its value when the works were completed would be £1,900, and the County Court judge held that the works could not therefore be carried out at reasonable expense. In the Court of Appeal it was held that since the value of the property on the open market before and after the completion of the works had been agreed by the parties, the judge's decision had been correct; though the statute did not prohibit the courts from having regard to other considerations in particular cases in borderline cases, there was no ground for introducing such factors in such a clear case; nor was there any ground for going into the different permissible methods of arriving at the open market value where figures had been agreed.

This rule applies whether or not vacant possession can be offered to a potential buyer. Accordingly where a house is occupied by tenants protected by the Rent Acts, the open market value can only be the "investment value," that is the amount which might be obtained on the open market on the assumption that the tenancy will continue:

Bacon v. *Grimsby Corporation (1950)*

A local authority served notices on a leaseholder of a number of tenanted houses, requiring him to carry out certain works to render the houses fit. The leases on the houses had 12 and 21 years to run. The tenants were protected under the Rent Acts and paid about 50p per week. The leaseholder appealed on the ground that the local authority had not considered detailed estimates of the cost of the works and that the works could not be carried out at reasonable expense in relation to his interest as leaseholder. The Court of Appeal held that the local authority was not bound to consider detailed estimates of the cost of the works and the value of the houses before issuing such notices, and that if the issue were raised by the person on whom the notices were served the relevant value was the freehold value of the houses, on the basis that they contained tenants protected under the Rent Acts.

3. *Methods of Valuation*

Acceptance of these general principles does not of itself resolve the application of the reasonable expense criterion in individual cases. The only specific guidance on the proper method of valuation which has been given by the Court of Appeal is the suggestion in *Kimsey* v. *Barnet London Borough Council* that the value of unfit premises which would have to be closed if the required works were not done cannot exceed the site value. This suggestion, however, cannot be reconciled with the judgements in the many other cases decided in the Court of Appeal and elsewhere in which a specific investment value far above the site value has been fixed for unfit premises; it must accordingly be taken at best to be limited to the special circumstances of that case in that the unfit premises were part only of the building, and more probably to be an error which was not crucial to the outcome of the case before the court. In other cases the courts have been unwilling to prescribe any particular method of valuation. Local authorities may therefore adopt a number of different approaches.

The simplest and safest method is that of comparable sales. In simple term this means that the value of the house is estimated from actual market sales of similar properties. This works well and is generally acceptable where there is an active market in properties of the relevant type from which simple adjustments for the state of repair and for general price movements can be made. Open market sales, however, are frequently limited to houses offered with vacant possession for owner occupation. Sales of tenanted properties for investment are much less frequent, not least because few investors are prepared to purchase properties with sitting tenants who are protected by the Rent Acts. What sales there are of such properties are likely to be forced sales on the death of the owner, and it is accordingly arguable that the price fetched may not be a true reflection of value.

To surmount this difficulty a number of alternative methods have been developed through which a capital value may be derived from rental income. The best known of these, sometimes referred to as Swift's method, is based upon a number of years' purchase of the net annual income from the property (S. Swift, *Housing Administration* (1958), Ch. 13). The annual return is calculated from the gross rental income, less appropriate percentages for management and repair costs. The multiplier may then be taken to be a constant, for instance twelve times the net annual return. Alternatively it may be derived from current interest rates in order to produce an appropriate capitalisation of annual yield; for instance if interest rates are about 8 per cent the appropriate multiplier would be $12\frac{1}{2}$, while if interest rates were about 10 per cent the multiplier would be 10. The special nature of tenancies controlled or regulated under the Rent Acts, however, produce equally serious problems in this context as for the comparable sales method. In the first place it is highly unrealistic to take management and repair costs to be a fixed percentage of gross rental income. The standard allowance of about 25 per cent of gross income rarely produces sufficient in the case of rent-controlled properties even for regular maintenance, let alone the more expensive repairs and renewals which are required from time to time in older properties. If a realistic sum is allowed for repairs, on the other hand, the net return and therefore the notional valuation may be reduced to virtually nothing. In the second place the method takes no account of the prospect of obtaining vacant possession at some time in the future. It is notorious that there is a substantial difference between the value of a property with vacant possession and its value with a sitting tenant. It follows that the market price for the property, if there were a market, would not be based solely on the annual income but also on the anticipated expiration of the statutory tenancy on the death

of the occupant or by a voluntary termination in return for a
lump sum payment; less scrupulous landlords may also be able
to winkle the tenant out by less acceptable and lawful pressures. The market value of the property will therefore lie
somewhere between the "pure" investment value, assuming
that the tenancy will continue indefinitely, and the value with
immediate vacant possession, and will vary according to the
personal circumstances and age of the tenant. For these
various reasons no mathematical formula based on current
rental income can produce a satisfactory guide to the true
value of tenanted properties. The higher courts, however, have
not encouraged local authorities to take factors of this kind
into account in assessing reasonable expense. When the matter
was raised in *Inworth Property Co.* v. *London Borough of
Southwark* (1977) (above) the Court of Appeal held that the
statutory requirement to have regard to the value of the
property when the works were completed did not exclude the
local authority from having regard to other factors, but that
those other factors could not alter the basic requirement to
have regard to the open market value; and that in the circumstances of the case, in which the open market value had been
agreed by the parties, evidence could not be brought to show
that value meant something other than open market value.
This leaves open the possibility of introducing evidence of the
anticipated continuation of the tenancy as a guide to the
proper market value, but such evidence is rarely taken into
account in practice.

4. *The Reasonable Expense Criterion under the Housing Act 1974*

The difficulties in applying the precise terms of the reasonable
expense criterion eventually led to pressures to remove the
requirement under the Housing Act 1957, s. 39 that in assessing reasonable expense regard should be had to the value
which the house will have when the prescribed works are completed. When the provisions governing compulsory improvement notices under the Housing Act 1964, which originally
involved an identical reasonable expense criterion to that
under the Housing Act 1957, were re-enacted under the

Housing Act 1974, ss. 85 and 89 this requirement was purposely omitted. The Department of the Environment then advised local authorities that while the interpretation of reasonable expense was ultimately a matter for the courts on appeal, the removal of the restrictive requirement in earlier statutes meant that "a local authority is ... free to have regard to any matters which it considers to be relevant." (Circular 160/74, Appendix E, para. 2.)

The precise legal effect of this omission has yet to be determined in the higher courts. But the terms of Circular 160/74 have been relied on by some local authorities in support of improvement notices which might not have been permissible under earlier legislation. The issue has also come before the county courts in a number of areas. In some cases the judges have in effect applied the same rules as under earlier statutes: in *W. & J. Venmore* v. *Metropolitan Borough of Sefton* (1976), the judge held that where, from a comparison of the value before and after the completion of the improvement, it appeared that the landlord would have to spend some £2,300 and £1,500 (after allowing for grant aid) to achieve enhancements of some £500 and £800, the proposed expenditure was clearly unreasonable. In other cases the judges have moved away from a strict assessment of enhanced value and have taken other factors into account to enable the proposed expenditure to be held reasonable where it would clearly not have been so under the old rules. In *Harris* v. *Lewisham London Borough Council* (1976), where the cost to the landlord of carrying out the prescribed improvements was assessed at some £700 and there was a certificate from the Rent Officer that the fair rent should be increased from £7.50 to £8.00, the judge held that the fact that the tenant was aged 65 and had no successor living with her and that the execution of the works would increase the life of the property by some ten years were both relevant factors and that in all the circumstances the expense to the owner was reasonable. Similarly in *Perks* v. *Middlesborough Borough Council* (April 1976), though the cost of the prescribed improvements (some £800) was less than the estimated enhancement of the value of the property (from some £450 to some £1,275) and there was to be an increase in rent from £1.13 to £3.80, the judge held that given the overall context of the Housing Act 1974 "reasonable expense" had to be construed in a wider context than mere financial expediency; though the rent was being held at an unrealistically low level, the landlord might eventually gain possession and be able to realise the full open market value of some £4,000; if the landlord did not wish to carry out the prescribed works his remedy was to serve a purchase notice on the local authority; the Act was strong in its intention that "come what may houses lacking standard amenities must be improved." In both these cases, it should be noted, the judges have taken explicit account of the substantial difference between the investment value with a sitting tenant and the open market value with vacant possession. It is arguable that the chances of obtaining vacant possession in such cases should be taken into account in a true assessment of the investment value, so that there is no inherent conflict of approach. But it is clear that some county court judges have made a point of applying a more liberal test than under the statutes of 1957 and 1964.

5. *The Criterion of Reasonableness under the Housing Act 1957, s. 9(1A)*

When the repair notice procedure in respect of unfit houses was extended to houses which are fit but in substantial disrepair under the Housing Act 1969 the reasonable expense criterion was omitted altogether. But local authorities may only prescribe such repairs as are "reasonable in relation to the age, character and locality of the property" (Housing Act 1957, s. 9(1A), as substituted by the Housing Act 1969, s. 72). This formulation, which is also adopted as a condition for certain grants (see Chapter 5), appears to permit local authorities to require owners to bring their houses up to a reasonable standard without regard to strict financial criteria. But similar considerations to those involved under the formal reasonable expense criterion have in practice been raised in many of the cases in which owners have appealed against repair notices. In a number of areas owners have successfully appealed against notices served under section 9(1A) on the simple ground that the repairs prescribed by the local authority are either unnecessary or excessive or that the house in question is in better general condition than others in the area. But financial as opposed to purely physical criteria have also been taken into account in many cases. This approach has recently been approved by the Court of Appeal:

> *Hillbank Properties Ltd. v. Hackney London*
> *Borough Council (1978)*
>
> A local authority served repair notices under s. 9(1A) in respect of two houses, each owned by a separate property company. Each company appealed against the notice on the ground that it was unreasonable to require it to carry out the prescribed works. The county court judge found that the cost of the repairs for one of the houses would be £2,750, that its value with a sitting tenant in an unrepaired state was £1,700, that its value with a sitting tenant after the repairs would be £2,300, and that its value after the repairs with vacant possession would be £7,500; the position in respect of the second house was similar; he quashed the notices on the ground that the cost of the works was greater than the increase in the value of the houses with sitting tenants. The Court of Appeal allowed an appeal by the local authority: it was held that the county court could properly take into account the cost of the works and the resulting increase in the value of the property, along with any other relevant considerations, but that the judge had erred in taking the value of the houses to be their value with sitting tenants; he should have taken into account the prospect that the landlord might obtain vacant possession and accordingly should have taken their value to be the vacant possession value or at least a figure between that and the value with a sitting tenant; on that basis the repair notices were reasonable; the fact that if the houses were allowed to deteriorate, the landlord might gain vacant possession when they became statutorily unfit was also relevant.

An appeal against this decision to the House of Lords has been abandoned. Until it is reversed or altered by statute, it seems clear that financial criteria may properly be taken into account in any appeal against a repair notice under s. 9(1A). It is much less clear what test is to be used for the valuation of tenanted properties. It would appear from the judgements in the Court

of Appeal that county courts may take the value to be that with
vacant possession if there is any immediate prospect of the
landlord gaining vacant possession, but that otherwise it
should be taken to be investment value, including any longer
term prospect of obtaining vacant possession.

6. *An Alternative Running Expenditure Criterion*

The difficulties which have been experienced in applying the
various reasonable expense criteria have led some local
authorities to question the need for any reasonable expense
criterion at all. Unless local authorities and courts are to be
given absolute freedom to require all owners to spend whatever is necessary to bring their houses up to a given physical
standard, however, some such criterion must be found, if only
as a guide to the proper exercise of a statutory discretion. The
difficulty with the current approach is that in focusing attention on capital values it raises issues which are almost impossible to resolve in cases involving rented properties with
controlled or regulated rents. The divergence between investment value with a sitting tenant and free market value with
vacant possession in such cases often makes it extremely difficult to decide what landlords can reasonably be expected to
spend on repairs.

An alternative approach, which avoids the problems of
attempting to fix a capital value for such properties is to tie the
reasonable expense criterion to the *current* income and expenditure of landlords from their properties. The general principle
that owners should not be required to comply with schemes for
compulsory rehabilitation if they will be seriously out of pocket
on a short term or a long term basis as a result should not be
altered. But attention should be focused on the financing of that
part of the prescribed works which cannot be grant aided. Thus
where the additional income to a landlord from an increase in
rent is sufficient to meet the cost of financing any necessary loan
over the period for which he may be required to give a certificate
of continued letting for grant purposes, the expenditure would
be reasonable; where there is no additional income or where it
would be less than sufficient to meet the loan charges and
repayments, the expenditure would be unreasonable.

This formulation allows a good deal of flexibility to local authorities. Where an authority wishes to enforce costly rehabilitation and there is a limit on the amount of centrally funded grant-aid, then the authority could bring the scheme within the reasonable expenditure criterion by extending the term of the loan or making a discretionary addition to the grant. For example, if a rehabilitation scheme was costed at £10,000 and the increase in rental income to the landlord as a result was only £10 per week, the landlord's reasonable expenditure on the scheme would be about £500 per year; with a standard grant of 50 per cent or £5,000, this would be sufficient only to meet current interest charges of 10 per cent; the local authority might then either offer a maturity loan, charging the capital sum against the deeds of the property, or else make an additional discretionary grant. It would thus be open to an authority to fix the terms of any loan offered to the landlord to meet the new criterion. The landlord would not be bound to accept those terms; but if he refused, he would then have to raise alternative finance himself.

This test for reasonable current expenditure might be adopted either as a *replacement* or as an *alternative* to the existing enhanced value test which operates reasonably effectively for owner-occupier or vacant properties for which there is an effective open market. In legal terms the test might be formulated as follows:

> Expenditure for the purpose of compulsory rehabilitation notices in respect of tenanted properties shall be deemed to be reasonable where the additional annual income to the owner as a result of the rehabilitation equals or exceeds the annual cost to the owner of interest and capital repayments on the loan which the local authority is required to offer under section ...

It should perhaps be added that there is already a requirement on local authorities to make loans for the purposes of compulsory improvement notices under section 100 of the Housing Act 1974, so that no new principle of public finance would be involved in the adoption of the new test.

INDEX